First published in 1995 in Great Britain
by Bewick Press, Tyne & Wear NE26 3TX

This edition, 2011
by Unkant Publishing
First Floor Offices, Hoxton Point, 6 Rufus Street, London N1 6PE

© 1995 Raymond Challinor
The right of Raymond Challinor to be identified as the author of this work
has been asserted in accordance with the Copyright, Designs and Patents Act
1998.

Designed by Keith Fisher
Cover illustration by Ben Watson
British Library Cataloguing-in-Publication Data
A CIP catalogue record for this book is available from the British Library
A Paperback Original
ISBN 978-0-9568176-1-7
1 3 5 7 9 10 8 6 4 2

Set in Unkant Jensen
www.unkant.com

The Struggle for Hearts and Minds
Essays on the Second World War

Ray Challinor

Unkant Publishing
London, UK

Ray Challinor

Ray Challinor (1929–31 January 2011) was a member of
the Independent Labour Party, the Labour Party and the
Trotskyist movement. He was a founder of the Socialist
Review Group (later the International Socialists and
Socialist Workers Party) in 1950 and edited its journal for
several years. He participated in the anti-nuclear campaign
and belonged to the Committee of 100. For a period in the
1960s he was a councillor in Newcastle-under-Lyme on the
Labour Party ticket, in which party IS was then resident,
later writing an article in *International Socialism* on how the
experience was politically dispiriting. Born in Stoke-on-
Trent, he was educated at Keele and Lancaster Universities
and became principal lecturer in History at Newcastle
Polytechnic. While a member of the Socialist Workers
Party, he wrote his best known work, a classic history of
the Socialist Labour Party, *The Origins of British Bolshevism*
(1977). He served as Chairman of the Society for the Study
of Labour History and President of the North East Labour
History Society. A well-known historian, among the books
he has written are *The Miners' Association: A Trade Union in
the Age of the Chartists*, *The Origins of British Bolshevism*, *John
S. Clarke: Parliamentarian, Poet and Lion-tamer* and *A Radical
Lawyer in Victorian England: W.P. Roberts and the Struggle for
Workers' Rights*.

Credits

Some of these essays first appeared in the following magazines: *Critique, ILP News, International Socialism, Workers' Liberty,* and *Workers' Press.* One was written as long ago as 1972, when the political climate as quite different. It is republished here because, amid the patriotic frenzy associated with the fiftieth anniversary of the end of the Second World War, it contains information that otherwise may be forgotten.

Cartoons

The cartoons were published in *Forward* (p. 73), *New International* (p. 21), *War Commentary* (pp. 46, 78, 83), *Plebs* (pp. 18, 108), *Socialist Appeal* (p. 50), *New Leader* (pp. 76, 90).

Contents

Preface

Ray Challinor's book, first published in 1995, makes a crucial contribution to the history of the Second World War. It uncovers a deliberately hidden history of the war that shatters the comforting narratives that have been spun around the cataclysm.

We weren't 'all in it together'. How deeply, 'in it' you found yourself was straightforwardly determined by which social class you were born into, or which 'race' you were deemed to be a member of. Nor was it a war for democracy against tyranny. The various members of the world's ruling classes switched allegiances with one another before, during and immediately after the conflict with bewildering speed and ease. Growing intelligence on the concentration camps was dismissed; civilian safety was treated as an annoying afterthought; Franco's fascist dictatorship survived untouched and undisturbed. If there is something familiar about the patterns that emerge in the book it is because many of the features of selling wars to recalcitrant populations, demonising enemies and eradicating dissent were systematically matured during the conflict, on all sides.

Alongside the unique view of various forms of resistance to war, Challinor also exposes those members of the ruling class who dramatically benefitted from the mechanisation of carnage. Aside from the obvious benefits to armament manufacturers and materials speculators there were the obscene differences in daily life. During the aerial bombardments of London it was possible to travel from the Dorchester Hotel, replete with bomb-proof luxury suites, personal waiters and games rooms, to the Isle of Dogs, where you would find 8,000 people crammed into filthy warehouses sharing eight toilets every night.

Then there was the nomenclature of fear – that remains with us – where 'threat levels' were organised into comfortable associations with traffic lights: red, amber (a more poetic encoding than today's 'orange') and green for all-clear. Except that even the colours had to be appended to keep production going. It was deemed far too disruptive to output to have workers scatter for shelter during every air raid so, 'purple' was mixed into the palette. A 'purple' alert meant the following: 'Your workplace is in the direct line of flight of enemy bombers. However, we have completed a risk assessment and are confident that you should simply continue running the machines...'

Challinor's book does not simply remain at the level of sociological categories; it deals with the dreadful consequences of the war for individuals. The execution of George Armstrong, the first British citizen hanged for spying, is presented as one of the first of many miscarriages of justice and relayed with particular evidence showing how murderous sections of Britain's secret state apparatus was. Armstrong was a merchant seaman, had loose ties to the Independent Labour Party (ILP) and was most likely aware of, if not directly involved in, the growing discontent among sailors. The mass protest meetings of merchant seamen in Baltimore and Boston are not recorded in most armchair-generalship manuals that pass for history today.

Indeed, Ray Challinor approached this project as a lifelong socialist whose first political experiences were had at the outbreak of war. His parents, both socialist teachers, introduced him to the ILP and helped expose him to the thin red line of anti-Stalinist militants who were principled opponents of the drive to war. Their stories are told here along with the efforts of anarchist, community activist and underground press networks. He also details the significant impact revolutionary socialist and anarchist ideas had among rank and file members of the armed forces.

The account's overall approach has to be put into the context of a world in which the opposition to war could have been expected to emerge from the mass European Communist parties. After all, the Russian Revolution had occurred in living memory for many and its success had ended the slaughter of the First World War. However, the Revolution's isolation and ultimate defeat enabled Stalin to invert both the gains and the impulse of the original Bolshevik victory.

The inversion was completed in 1939 with the Ribbentrop-Molotov pact. The neck-breaking turns enforced on 'satellite' communist parties played a vital role in ensuring fascism's rise and eventual victory in Spain, Italy and Germany. The switching between opposition then alliance with fascist states effectively disabled any effective opposition to the rise of Nazism in Europe.

And yet, despite this grim history, resistance persisted in the form of Trotskyist and anarchist cadres struggling to reinstate an anti-imperialist perspective throughout the late 1920s and 30s. The world's rulers were fully attuned to the threat these traditions posed. Three days after the signing of the non-aggression pact between Stalin's Russia and Nazi Germany, Robert Coulondre, the French ambassador in Berlin interviewed Hitler:

> **Coulondre**: *The real victor in case of war will be Trotsky. Have you thought that over?*
> **Hitler**: *I know. I know.*

It is the immanent threat posed by 'ordinary people' to each and every ruler's war aims that Challinor's book conveys so well. Alongside the wealth of material chronicling organised resistance – Britain's Peace Pledge Union alone had over 100,000 paying members – there are the insights into the mass 'spontaneous' self-organisation that existed. Alfie Bass's London Underground Station and Shelterers' Committee was born out of the refusal to open tube stations to civilians. It took riots, in which two men were killed, in Portsmouth to open access to shelters and squatters associations became so widespread, after nearly 40 percent of the housing stock had been destroyed, that the Home Office simply gave up on evictions.

We now find ourselves, at the beginning of the 21st century, in a world in which two major wars of occupation are still being fought in Iraq and Afghanistan, the world's financial system has gone through its worst crisis since the 1930s, and where governments have discovered the need for 'austerity' for most while a minority stretch the concept of 'obscene wealth' to its breaking-point.

There are also revolutions! The Middle East, a minor part of Churchill's napkin note to Stalin as they carved up the planet at the war's end, is experiencing social upheavals that are squarely rooted in the Second World War's outcome. These revolutions – from Tunisia, Egypt, Libya, Syria, Bahrain, Yemen and beyond – are pointers, just as the Bolsheviks were in 1917, to how war can be permanently eradicated. Ray Challinor's book is a necessary tool for those both inspired by that vision and in forging that type of world.

Ray Challinor died in January 2011, and this edition of one of his most important books is dedicated to his memory and the tradition and the revolutionary socialist perspectives he fought for a lifetime to preserve.

Keith Fisher, v-2011

The Struggle for Hearts and Minds

'And so, comrades, we are agreed to compensate Luxemburg with
a piece of Paraguay, Paraguay with a piece of Timbuktu, and public
opinion with another statement of peace aims.'

The Nature of Conflict

To go to war is to take a step into the unknown. It remains rarely, if ever, possible to predict the outcome with certainty. Almost always surprises pop up. Unexpectedly, small Finland inflicted grievous hurt on the Soviet Union in the winter of 1939. A few months later everyone was amazed – the German generals included – by the speed with which the Allied armies in France crumbled. The following year, as the German invasion of Russia achieved such spectacular initial success, most experts believed Stalin would soon sue for peace. And so one could go on.

Most readers of history books forget a vital fact about the Second World War: they possess the privilege of viewing events after the outcome has been established. They do not have the agony of the characters in the drama at the time, having to make the decisions, dithering about what to do – and unsure what the consequences of their actions will be. This can be shown by examining the number of occasions war leaders' predictions proved to be wrong. In 1940, after Dunkirk, Hitler believed the British government, realising the hopelessness of the situation, would sue for peace. Again, in 1941 Hitler thought that the destruction of men and material which had been inflicted on the Soviet Union was so grievously immense, further resistance by the Red Army would be impossible. As a consequence, Germany could start to demobilise and reconvert its economy once more to peace. The Führer did not imagine how the conflict would ultimately end, with him beleaguered in his bunker, enemy armies closing in around Berlin, and his only alternative to humiliating capture being that of suicide. Nor could Mussolini, out to rekindle the glories of ancient Rome, ever envisage the adventure would end with him and his mistress, dead and hung upside down, surrounded by resistance fighters defiling their corpses.

It is tempting to make the analogy with a football match: the historian and his readers evaluate the struggle after the ball has been kicked for the last time. By contrast, the war leader is akin to the manager before the kick off: he doesn't know whether his plans with work; he does not know what the ultimate outcome will be. But such a comparison does not fully express the degree of uncertainty: in the Second World War, another mighty country might enter the conflict on this or that side, completely altering the balance of forces. It would be as if a football team playing Arsenal suddenly to its horror found Liverpool were also playing against them as well.

There remains another crucial difference. In football the winner is whichever side scores the most goals. The victor in a war is not necessarily the one that achieves the highest body-count, the greatest number of kills. Rather it goes to whichever side has the greater endurance and tenacity, willing to continue the conflict when its opponent has no stomach for further fight. It is as if a football match continued until one of the teams fell down, so exhausted it could play no longer.

In the Second World War Germany slaughtered more of the Allied military personnel in Europe that the Allies did in reply. Likewise in the Far East: Japan possessed the most efficient mass murder machine. But this did not mean Germany and Japan were the winners. They lost because the will to fight had evaporated, with soldiers raising their hands to surrender, not to fire a gun. It had been an endurance contest, a struggle to see which side was the first to say: 'Enough. We surrender'.

Paradoxically, politicians declare war in order to secure peace – but, crucially, peace on their own terms. Similarly, soldiers take up arms in order to put them down again. To state it in terms of Vera Lynne's song, sweetheart of the British forces in the Second World War, they want to see "bluebirds over the white cliffs of Dover" – in other words, an end to all hostilities, a return to civvy street. But the big question remains: how is this supremely sought after aim to be attained? It is an aim that can only be achieved when the enemy has been persuaded to alter its behaviour.

Warfare, in the final analysis, is a struggle for hearts and minds. The thud of bombs and shells is merely a noisy orchestral accompaniment of a process to achieve this desired end-result – that of altering the conduct of the other side, making an enemy submissive to one's will. What happened in November 1944 illustrates this point. Dr Goebbels made a series of impassioned speeches, telling German civilians that the Russian barbarians were at the gates, their national survival was in peril, and urging them to volunteer for the Volksturm – the Nazi equivalent of Britain's Home Guard. Old men and young boys enthusiastically volunteered. A few months later, however, the tattered remnant of Germany's Dad's Army, tired and much wiser, queued up to enter the prisoner-of-war camps. Accompanying them were entire regiments of the Wehrmacht. Hitler's deputy, Martin Bormann, admitted half a million men had deserted the armed forces. Organised resistance had collapsed: the war was over.

It would seem to me that most military historians make a conceptual error. Almost all their attention is devoted to the actual fighting. What they should make central to their accounts is why people stop fighting. It is only when this happens that a battle or war has been lost and won. Victory arrives once military personnel begin acting in a non-military manner – that is they say, 'Enough is enough. We will stop fighting'.

Admittedly, military historians discuss what makes one group of men an efficient fighting force, better than another's. Equally, they may state how battle-exhaustion may cause a body of men to act less effectively or even become demoralised. Rarely, if ever, however, do they ponder to consider the reasons for soldiers refusing to fight. Yet, in conflict there are sometimes those who refuse, despite the personal danger to themselves, to slay individuals who are supposed to be their enemy.

In 1943-5, American Colonel S.L.A. Marshall inquired into how US troops behaved under fire. Amazingly, he found that only 15% of trained combat riflemen fired their weapons in battle. Even in the most aggressive infantry companies, the figure rarely rose above 25%. The rest did not flee, but they would not kill. It still remained true when their positions were under enemy attack and their own lives in danger. This did not happen because, in the heat of battle, they somehow forgot their training. Make a soldier part of a crew, say, manning an artillery battery, and the required duties will usually be performed. Troubles arise when the soldier is alone, isolated from others in battalion and having to act on his own initiative. Colonel Marshall suggests a possible explanation:

> *It is therefore reasonable to believe that the average and healthy individual – the man who can endure the mental and physical stresses of combat – still has such an inner and usually unrealised resistance towards killing a fellow man that he will not of his own volition take life if it is possible to turn away from the responsibility... At a vital point he becomes a conscientious objector, unknowingly.*

Colonel Marhall's research was quoted by Dr Dwynne Dyer, a senior lecturer at Royal Military Academy, Sandhurst, who produces a television series based upon his book, entitled *War*. His own work, Dr Dyer states, confirm these findings: "Men will kill under compulsion... but the vast majority of men are not born killers". In battles, the volume of fire would be three, four or five times greater had everybody enthusiastically joined in.

Modern warfare makes it virtually impossible for commanding officers to maintain close supervision of troops in battle. The sheer volume of firepower an enemy could concentrate on a small area means dispersal remains essential for survival. Yet, with dispersal soldiers get spaced out over a larger distances and supervision grows less and less effective. The scope for the 'pacifist' private soldiers becomes greater.

The heads of all present-day armies are secretly aware of this problem. It leads them to keep the closest surveillance possible of the troops under their command. In the First World War, the British Expeditionary Force opened and censored all letters. It also sought to gauge the morale of the men, plotting on a graph the changes, from what they wrote to their families back home. The same happened in the Second World War. Those likely to damage other soldiers' fighting spirit were discreetly weeded out. But however elaborate the procedures, the top brass realise its control always remains fragile. An unexpected event could easily destroy the willingness not only of the individual soldier but also the entire army to continue to struggle. An epidemic of defeatism can quickly ravage regiment after regiment.

This was what happened to the British Expeditionary Force (BEF) once the German panzer divisions had penetrated Allied lines in May 1940. The first response of the BEF was to move across the river Dyle. Then, in panic, they soon engaged the troops on the other bank in the battle. These turned out not to be Germans at all, but friendly Allied troops, the hapless 10th Belgian division. Not having acquitted themselves with glory in that encounter, for the rest of the campaign the British army mainly confined itself to retreating in disorder to the port of Dunkirk. Almost all the fighting was done by the French and Belgians. As Winston Churchill frankly told the British commander, General Gort: "Of course, when one side fights and the other does not, the war is apt to be somewhat unequal".

To understand why the Dunkirk disaster happened, it is necessary to investigate all the underlying influences – the ineptitude of the British army high command, the British government's half-hearted prosecution of the war, the numerous surreptitious peace negotiations with Nazi Germany, etc. All these must have had an effect on the British Tommy's morale, making him question whether he should be prepared to recklessly lay down his life. Nothing appeared worth fighting for in 1930s Britain. If lucky, he would return to the slum house, the dole queue, the poverty. Why kill other human beings so you might return to such appalling conditions?

Everybody knows von Clausewitz's famous dictum that "war is politics by other means"; many less have pondered over its implications. At all junctures, political considerations underpin the military action. The reasons why wars are fought, in the first place, are political. The manner in which war is fought remains, in the last analysis, political. And, finally, the reason why the conflict is ended are political. In other words, as von Clausewitz asserted, military grammar must be subordinated to political logic.

All this means I make no apology for writing this book. Conflict remains a struggle for hearts and minds. Once one side loses the fighting spirit, indeed surrenders, then war is over.

The Second World War and its Hidden Agenda

Emrys Hughes, son-in-law of Keir Hardie, edited the *Glasgow Forward*, an independent socialist weekly. He was proud of his connection with such an important pioneer of the Labour Movement. He preserved the small miner's cottage at Cummock in Ayrshire, where Hardie had lived, as if it were in a time-capsule. The great man's memory needed to be perpetuated. But Emrys Hughes had another hero – Leon Trotsky. Emrys Hughes boasted that "for a long time *Forward* was the only newspaper in Britain that dared to publish articles from Trotsky". Emrys Hughes' papers, housed in the National Library of Scotland, contain letters from Trotsky, from his son, Leon Sedov, and from his secretary, Joseph Hansen, as well as two gramophone records of Trotsky's speeches. Not surprisingly, on April 3rd, 1939 Emrys Hughes wrote to Trotsky. He wanted to discover first hand Trotsky's reactions to the deepening world crisis.

In his letter, Hughes realistically acknowledged the approach of war. Its outbreak, he predicted, would initially trigger off a gigantic wave of patriotic fervour, just as the 1914-18 had done: "I hardly think it will be possible for an anti-war socialist paper to survive during the first stage of war hysteria". But he remained undismayed. The immense death and destruction caused by the conflict would eventually be intolerable to the masses. His letter continued:

> *I entirely agree with your analysis that a "new world war will provoke with absolute inevitability the world revolution and the collapse of the capitalist system". The world war will unleash tremendous forces, especially in western capitalist countries... It will end in chaos out of which there will come a great demand for peace and fundamental change.*

In his reply, written on April 22nd, 1939, Trotsky said there were thousands of British workers and revolutionary intellectuals who thought like Emrys Hughes did: "They are simply stifled, but not so much by the state machine as the machine of the official workers' organisations". The war currently being prepared, Trotsky thought, would sweep aside these impediments to progress, making revolution the inevitable outcome of the conflict.[1]

Both Emrys Hughes and Trotsky miscalculated. They were wrong on two of their three prophecies. Though correct in forecasting the coming world conflict, this amounted to no great feat: as the Thirties staggered from disaster to disaster, a pervasive feeling grew up that an international conflict could not be long delayed. But their other two forecasts – initial patriotic frenzy and ultimate revolution – did not arise from the smoke of battle. This illustrates an important lesson: while it is true those who do not learn the lessons of the past are condemned to repeat the errors of the past, nevertheless applying these lessons remains an exceedingly difficult procedure. Even a brilliant brain like Trotsky can be wrong, simplistically anticipating the past to repeat itself mechanically, not appreciating the complex new forces at work, creating an entirely different end-result. A further complicating factor may be the ruling class, itself having acquired experience and knowledge from battles of yester-year, may be unwilling to sit back and passively witness its own destruction. It may take precautionary measures in an attempt to avert revolution happening.

For various reasons, the outbreak of the Second World War was not a re-run of the outbreak of the First World War. By 1939, the public in all the major countries had the horrors of the First World War etched into their collective memory. Virtually nobody believed it would be a question of young men doing a few heroic deeds and then returning home to recount their exploits with their families over Christmas dinner. Rather it was recognised war would be a protracted struggle, resulting in millions of dead, large numbers maimed, immense suffering. Hence the carnival atmosphere of 1914 was absent in 1939. War fever did not silence the dissenters. The general response of the public in all the belligerent countries differed greatly from this forecast.

On September 3rd 1939, William L. Shirer, the American journalist, strolled around the German capital. A lot of people, taking advantage of the warm, sunny day, were wandering around the parks. Shirer found the average Berliner reacted to the news that war had just been declared without enthusiasm:

> *In 1914, I believe, the excitement in Berlin on the first day of the World War was tremendous. Today, no excitement, no hurrahs, no cheering, no throwing of flowers, no war fever, no war hysteria. There is not even any hate for the French and British despite Hitler's various proclamations to the people. I walked in the streets. On the faces of the people astonishment, depression.*[2]

The German armies' spectacularly quick victory over Poland did not dispel the prevailing gloom. Realistically, even the military themselves conceded the deep

---

1. *Writings of Leon Trotsky 1938-39*, New York, Pathfinder Press, 1969, p. 308. Letter from Emrys Hughes to Leon Trotsky in Keir Hardie-Hughes papers in the National Library of Scotland. The Hardie-Hughes papers contain a number of letters from Trotsky, his son Leon Sedov and his secretaries. See Raymond J. Ross, 'Trotsky among the Scots', in the literary magazine *Cencrastus*, Winter 1987-8.
2. William L. Shirer, *Berlin Diary* 1934-1941, London: Sphere, 1970, p. 159.

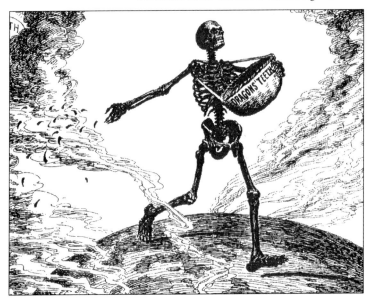

THE SOWER

feeling was one of public disenchantment. On October 3rd 1939, General Ritter von Leeb wrote in his diary:

> *Poor mood of the population, no enthusiasm at all, no flags flying from homes. Everyone waiting for peace. The people sense the needlessness of war.*[1]

Preparations had been made for a German attack on France and Belgium in October 1939, but it was called off because of the poor state of the Wehrmacht's morale. In the recently completed Polish campaign, disturbing symptoms had surfaced. Even David Irving, an historian with fascist sympathies, has to admit the German people had little passion for the war. In his biography of Hitler, Irving recounts a conversation the Führer had with the army commander who had been in charge of the recent invasion. General von Braushitch warned Hitler about the perilous state of army morale:

> *In the Polish campaign the infantry had shown little verve in attack, the general contended, and at times the NCOs and officers had lost control. Braushitch even spoke of 'mutinies' in some units, and he recounted acts of drunken indiscipline at the front and on the railways during the transfer west that invited comparison with the uglier scenes of 1917 and 1918.*[2]

---

1. Joachim C. Fest, *Hitler*, Penguin, 1977, p. 922.
2. David Irving, *Hitler's War 1939-1942*, Macmillan, 1983, p. 47. The 'ugliest' scenes of 1918 were, it should be remembered, mutiny and revolution.

The picture in Britain was very similar to Germany. There was little enthusiasm for the impending bloodbath. Organisations opposed to the war had, like Emyrs Hughes, expected to face massive waves of patriotic hostility. Accordingly, they had made contingency plans. Believing it essential to keep its leadership intact, the Trotskyist Workers' International League sent some of its leaders to neutral Ireland. It was hoped that from there it would be possible to re-establish links with whatever groups survived on the mainland. The ILP developed a plan to operate an illegal radio transmitter. The Communist Party also devised plans to circumvent the effects of state repression. These were partially implemented in 1941, when Herbert Morrison, the home secretary, banned the *Daily Worker*. Not believing in such centralism, the anarchists thought their decentralisation itself would afford some protection. The authorities would be unable to arrest all their supporters. Those fortunate enough to remain out of prison would continue to operate. It was to the initiative and enterprise of individuals that anarchism looked for its survival. Likewise, the Peace Pledge Union, with 140,000 members the largest anti-war organisation, made no provisions to combat governmental attacks. Most pacifists believed, if they were persecuted, their willingness to suffer for their principles would make people aware of the sincerity with which they held their convictions and perhaps provide the basis for greater public support.[1]

Much to their surprise, instead of being engulfed by a wave of jingoistic hysteria, anti-war organisations continued to function after the declaration of war. Not only that—they prospered! "The ILP is coming into its own again," declared its weekly paper, the *New Leader*. "The accession of new members is remarkable"' In the first six months after the outbreak of war, the ILP received 1,000 applications for membership.[2] It decided to increase its full-time staff, employing a further six regional organisers. The circulation of the pacifist weekly *Peace News* rose from 19,300 to 35,024 copies in the same period.[3] Most Trotskyist groups also expanded their size and influence.

There were also other manifestations of disenchantment. On March 15th, 1940, *Peace News* reported that 26,681 men had registered as conscientious objectors—in other words, in a mere six months the figure had reached almost half the total attained throughout the entire First World War. In the same month the National Union of Students' annual conference came out by 281 votes to 169 against the war. Performance of candidates opposed to the conflict in parliamentary by-elections fluctuated considerably. The nature of the constituency, the organisation (or lack of it) of the anti-war candidate, as

---

1. Douglas Hyde, 'Preparations for Illegality', *Our History Journal*, October 1989; P. J. Thwaites, The ILP 1938-1950, Ph.D., London School of Economics, 1976, pp. 103-4; Fenner Brockway, *Outside the Right*, Allen & Unwin, 1963, pp. 18-19; Sam Bornstein and Al Richardson, *War and the International*, Socialist Platform, 1986, p. 10; Caroline Moorehead, *Troublesome People: Enemies of War 1916-1986*, Hamish Henderson, 1987, pp. 145-150.
2. *New Leader*, March 29th, 1940, and ILP internal bulletin, *Between Ourselves*, December 1939 and February 1940.
3. *Peace News*, March 19th 1940.

well as the calibre of the person standing and the standpoint from which the government was attacked all influenced the outcome.

In December 1939, the ILP contested its first by-election, putting forward Bob Edwards at the Manchester constituency of Stretford. The Communist Party also decided to fight the seat. So, anyone disagreeing with the Government had a choice of two anti-war candidates. Bob Edwards, the ILP candidate, secured 4,424 votes while Eric Gower, the Communist candidate, gained 1,519 votes. At the 1935 general election, the Labour Party had obtained 35.6% of the votes cast. At the by-election four years later, it did not contest the seat as the Labour and Liberal Parties had agreed to accept a political truce. However, the combined votes of the ILP and Communist candidates meant that 20.2% of voters had opposed the war.

In Parliament on December 13th, 1939, Lord Arnold sought to chide the Government with the significance of the Stretford result. He compared it with the First World War, where peace candidates secured derisory votes at by-elections, such as at Stockton and South Aberdeen in March 1917, when the votes gained were 596 and 333 respectively. Yet at Stretford, without the electorate experiencing three years' hardship and sacrifices, nevertheless war weariness had reached levels never attained in the 1914-1918 conflict. Another by-election three months later at Kettering served to reinforce Lord Arnold's argument: William Ross, hurriedly assembling a scratch organisation and calling himself a 'Workers' and Pensioners' Anti-war Candidate', did still better. He gained 6,616 votes, more than a quarter of the vote of the successful Tory candidate, a patriotic army officer named Profumo.

Violent swings of opinion, however, characterise wars. Unexpected military defeats and victories cause volatility. Official propaganda always likes to depict rock-solid backing. Reality remains rather different, though political leaders are reluctant to acknowledge the fact. The changing fortunes of war cause violent fluctuations of mood. Likewise people finding themselves confronted by new situations, requiring the development of new responses, enhanced the degree of unpredictability. Instances abound that can be given from the first few months of the Second World War. What, for example, should your attitude be towards conscientious objection? In the same month – April 1940 – workers at the Platting Chair Company, Manchester, went on strike to secure the reinstatement of a colleague who was sacked because he refused to register for military service, while at a Yeovil glassworks the labour force had downed tools because they refused to work alongside a conscientious objector. And then there was the case of Private Kenneth Makin: he left prison still defiantly stating he would not do military service. To his fellow soldiers he was a hero: they cheered the courage he had shown, standing up to the brass-hats' bullying. To use the soldiers' parlance, he had demonstrated he was not prepared to eat chicken shit.[1]

Similar dissension arose inside the Labour Party. Its leader, Clement Attlee, endured continual heckling when he addressed the South Wales Labour Party

---

1. *New Leader*, April 4th 1940.

regional conference. The party managers sent Ellen Wilkinson, still with a left-wing reputation, to try and justify the Labour Party's pro-war line to the East Midland regional conference. Again, the speaker received a rough ride. At least, however, the party bosses succeeded in avoiding the clamour to have the matter put to a vote. Where that did occur, at the Labour Party's East Anglia regional conference, delegates voted anti-war by a three-to-one majority. Much worse was to happen in Scotland: so incensed were the 200 present at Stirling with what the platform were saying that the conference had to be abandoned after the three speakers–MPs Tom Johnson, Ellen Wilkinson and Arthur Woodburn–walked off the platform when they found the barracking too intense for them to continue. By March 1940, 90 Constituency Labour Parties had passed anti-war resolutions. Eighteen resolutions had been placed on the Labour Party annual conference agenda for consideration at Bournemouth in June 1940. A further 50 Constituency Labour Parties put motions down critical of the political truce arranged between the Labour leadership and the Tories.[1]

The platform could reasonably have expected a turbulent time. But it failed to materialise at Bournemouth. As already stated, violent shifts in public mood characterise all wars. In the early summer of 1940, German troops had just invaded the Low Countries. A wave of patriotism, akin to the hysteria that sometimes emerges during a soccer world cup, temporarily swept the country as British troops marched to their first serious engagement with the enemy. The Labour leaders were able to capitalise upon this at the annual conference. Yet, within two months, with the trouncing of the British Expeditionary Force in France and the humiliation of Dunkirk, deep cynicism and dark despair had descended again.

Behind the wild oscillations of opinion, there nevertheless remains an underlying constant factor, vital and asserting itself whatever the vicissitudes – namely, that society is a class divided society. In normal conditions, the working class remains at the bottom of the pile. It has the lowest income, the highest death rate, the poorest housing. Wars tend to disproportionately worsen the workers' position. Production necessarily is transferred from the manufacture of consumer goods to manufacturing weapons of war. In these circumstances of restricted supply, those who receive little are liable to receive still less. It is not merely that the working class has a lower income per head; under capitalism it also has less political power and less social status. Consequently, when it comes to the share out of scarce resources, workers and their families have less political muscle. They are liable to lose out.

In the Second World War, international socialists repeated what they had learned from their predecessors. They said that wars were terrible – they were terribly profitable. They quoted the German socialist, Rosa Luxemburg, who had in 1916 written, "As soldiers fall at the front, the profits of the arms manufacturers rise at home". For those living a generation later, the same argument was put in a slightly different form by John McGovern, MP. He bluntly told Parliament:

---

1. *Ibid.*

I say that in every war those who have encouraged young men to fight have themselves enjoyed immunity from the struggle. I have never seen the Cabinet battalions, the bishops' battalions, the landlords' battalions and the bankers' battalions going to the Front. All I have seen are miners' battalions, the artisans' battalions, the shopkeepers' battalions and the warehouse workers' battalions going to the Front in order to defend other people's rights and privileges.[1]

McGovern underlined his point when, on another occasion, he listened to the speech of a junior minister, Ellen Wilkinson. She had been telling Parliament and the country of her fervent support for the war. McGovern jumped up to inquire why, if she was so much in favour of the conflict, she had not joined the armed forces herself. She replied, "I am doing my job here"; to which McGovern's riposte came:

It is a damn good job. I can quite understand when people climb into that kind of job, at £30 or £40 a week, that they can ask the ordinary soldier to do his job for two shillings a day. That is the kind of sacrifice we are getting.[2]

Class tensions manifested themselves on the home front equally as in the armed forces. Ellen Wilkinson discovered this when, as junior minister at the Home Office, she helped to introduce compulsory fire watching. This was extremely unpopular. Though from the military standpoint factories needed protection during air raids, their owners usually lived in far away (and relatively safe) rural areas. Obviously, in the government's eyes, it would be wrong to expect them to journey the long way back merely to do their fire watching stint. Rather it should be the workers who guarded the bosses' factories. Yet, to workers, many of whom lived in houses close to factories, the potential targets, they thought that in an air raid it was more important to be at home, guarding their wives and children, not their employers' property. As a consequence, while five million individuals received papers ordering them compulsorily to fire watch, well over a million people claimed to be suffering from some illness or infirmity that made this a sheer impossibility. The government was placed in a quandary. The health services were already over-stretched. They simply did not have the doctors or nurses to conduct medical examinations on such a colossal scale. In a situation similar to the hiatus that arose more recently over the poll tax, the Home Office found itself powerless to ensure its own edict was carried out. Angrily, Ellen Wilkinson blurted out that it was a pity the British government did not have the same control over its subjects as Stalin had in the Soviet Union.

The Churchill government's inability to enforce obedience was a significant step along a dangerous path. Successful in their defiance on this question, would people go on to disregard other orders of the State? Would the authority of the authorities be undermined? That this will happen remains the ultimate nightmare for all war leaders. In John Reed's fine book, *Ten Days that Shook the World*, he gives a vivid illustration of when this process actually reaches the endgame. In Russia in October 1917, the Provisional Government resolved to

---

1. House of Commons, John McGovern, February 13th 1945.
2. *New Leader*, April 9th 1941.

issue a proclamation. But, as the cabinet discussion continued, ministers became increasingly aware that they were on their own. None of the troops, none of the sailors, would obey their commands. Instead they took them into the soldiers' and workers' councils. Aware that their power had ebbed away, ministers understood the futility of continuing their talks. John Reed reproduced the incomplete proclamation, along with the doodles of a hapless participant, in his book. The incomplete document remains an apt testament to the downfall of the Provisional Government and the emergence of Soviet power.

In any war, the leaders of the contending sides confront each other like two individuals, each sitting astride three-legged chairs. Hostilities continue until one of the other crashes to the ground because one of the legs have given way. What are these three legs, so essential to the war? The first, obviously, is the armed forces. Let them stop fighting, putting down their guns and voting for peace with their feet, and whatever the position in the rest the country, then the conflict cannot continue. Equally vital remains the second leg – the home front. Let the soldiers be eager to fight, this becomes impossible once the supplies of food and ammunition they require have dried up. The third, and final, leg remains the ruling class, the shadowy figures who stand behind the politicians, the persons who really take the vital decisions on war and peace. Let them calculate they stand to gain less by continuing the war than they do by ending it, and the war leaders, without these backers, inevitably go into free-fall.

But for the capitalist system, it can result in grave problems. Under the strains of conflict, all three legs may be seriously weakened. Traditional authority may well be undermined. In the chaos which ensues when links that bind class society reach breaking point, the spectre of revolution is liable to emerge. History provides many instances of conflicts culminating on the barricades. There is no evidence to suggest that the French people were in a particularly revolutionary mood in 1870. However, after the debacle of the French army at the hands of the Prussians, the working inhabitants of the capital rose up in rebellion. The Paris Commune gave to the world the first glimmer of what a socialist society would be like. Again, in 1905, after Tsarist Russia's military defeat by Japan, Russian workers and peasants took the process a stage further. In their revolution they created councils – the Russian word is 'soviet' – to be their instrument of class power, their means whereby Russia would be governed. Out of the First World War, still more spectacular progress came: a workers' state sprung up in Russia while elsewhere in Europe, including Germany, attempts to topple capitalism almost succeeded.

> *Who could say the same would not happen after the Second World War? The fear haunted the leaders of all the capitalist countries. A remarkable illustration of this comes from a conversation Hitler had with Robert Coulondre, the French ambassador to Germany. It occurred on August 25, 1939, three days after the Molotov-Ribbentrop non-aggression pact had been signed between Germany and the Soviet Union. Hitler told Coulondre he was proud of the agreement – he described it as "a realistic pact" – and went on to express his 'regrets' if it consequently led to French and German blood being spilled. "But,"*

> Coulondre objected, "Stalin displayed great double-dealing. The real victor in
> case of war will be Trotsky. Have you thought that over?' "I know," der Führer
> responded, "but why did France and Britain give Poland complete freedom of
> action?'"

The interview evoked a comment from Trotsky. His name had been used, he
said, because Hitler and Coulondre liked:

> to give a personal name to the spectre of revolution. But this is not the essence
> of this dramatic conversation: at the very moment when diplomatic relations
> were ruptured. 'War will inevitably provoke revolution,' the representative of
> imperialist democracy, himself chilled to the marrow, frightens his adversary.
> "I know," Hitler responds, as if it were a question decided long ago. "I know".
> Astonishing dialogue!
> Both of them, Coulondre and Hitler, represent the barbarism which advances
> over Europe. At the same time, neither of them doubt that their barbarism will
> be conquered by socialist revolution.[1]

In his assessment of Hitler, Trotsky misjudged the Nazi leader's thoughts on
the threat socialist revolution posed to his personal position. Admittedly, an
uprising in Germany might occur, but Hitler thought he could face the prospect with equanimity. Protected by a highly efficient repressive apparatus, he
believed any insurrection could be drowned in blood. He told his cronies he
would shoot "a batch of a few hundred thousand people". Hitler's favourite
saying, which he found humorous, was: "A dead man can no longer put up a
fight".[2]

In France, political leaders took a less relaxed approach. Everyone in the entire country remained conscious of the immense losses sustained in the First
World War. A lot of the fighting had happened on French soil. Consequently,
it had suffered large civilian and military casualties. Many of its finest cities
and factories had been destroyed. And all for what? Twenty years later, Germany, the rival it had vanquished at such tremendous cost, had again grown
stronger than France. No wonder many, even among France's top 60 families,
were in 1939 far from enthusiastically pro-war. There was, moreover, a big
French Communist Party. It followed the orders it received from Moscow. In
view of the German-Soviet non-aggression pact, the Communist Party leaders
were regarded very much as enemies in the camp. Many were imprisoned. The
Communist Party was declared illegal; its papers banned. Besides the communists, there were also influential members of the French Socialist Party and the
PSOP, the sister party of the ILP, which opposed the war.[3]

In summer 1940, as the German blitzkrieg gained momentum and the Allied
military position turned from bad to worse, it is hardly surprising the French
government, unsure of how much support it enjoyed in the country, became

---

1. *Paris-Soir*, August 31st 1939, quoted by Leon Trotsky, *In Defence of Marxism*, New
York: Pioneer Publishers, 1942, p. 32.
2. Joachim C. Fest, op. cit., p. 995.
3. Workers and Peasants' Socialist Party (*Parti Socialiste Ouvrier et Paysan*) – PSOP.

immensely alarmed. Paul Reynaud, the French prime minister, flew to London. He wanted to discuss the commitment of more British troops to the fight. Only if this was done, he told the cabinet, would there be a chance of averting complete collapse. But Paul Reynaud argued the menace came from an internal as well as an external threat. Among the notes he jotted down before he met British ministers was one that read: "Revolution both possible and probable – a factor ignored by your side". General Weygand, the French commander-in-chief, endorsed Reynaud's opinion. While more troops were essential to staunch the German advance, one thing was still more vital. Doubtless with the German breakthrough at Sedan in 1870 at the back of his mind, General Weygand had the spectre of a Paris Commune Mark Two before him. So he explained: "I still have fresh divisions. I intend to keep them to maintain order".[1]

Before the German onslaught, the French capitulated and sued for peace. German troops occupied most of the country, mainly the industrial areas. A relatively small, primarily agricultural region in southern France, retained nominal independence, with its head quarters at Vichy. Marshall Petain headed its neo-Nazi administration. A few stragglers from the defeated French army succeeded in reaching England. There, led by a then relatively unknown army officer named Charles de Gaulle, the Free French was formed. Hardly existing anywhere except on paper, the Free French remained small and isolated, scorned by the British hierarchy and held partly responsible for the recent military disaster.

Against this background, an intriguing meeting took place, on August 14th, 1940, at the French Embassy in London. Present were General de Gaulle, Marceau Pivert of the French PSOP and John McNair, General Secretary of the ILP. The aim was to explore the feasibility of co-ordinating action of revolutionary socialists and the Free French. From the outset of the discussion, Pivert and McNair conceded their objectives were mutually incompatible – de Gaulle wanted to see a capitalist France, they wanted a socialist France. Yet, both were anti-Hitler and sought to end Nazi occupation. Did not this provide the basis for some cooperation? Pivert cited what had happened in the Soviet Union early in 1918. Then, disregarding the pleas for peace emanating from the Kremlin, German troops continued their advance. So the Bolsheviks appealed to the French government for assistance, and their cries were heeded. French army personnel blew up bridges and disrupted enemy communications. The German's advance was slowed down, in places halted. As a result, the newly-created Soviet regime bought valuable time as did the French army on the Western Front. It meant that the Wehrmacht were unable to transfer troops from the East to participate in Ludendorff's spring offensive. In that crucial final campaign, the German army came within a bayonet's width of achieving final victory – in other words, winning the war – by knocking out France before the arrival of American troops in sufficient numbers gave the Allies decisive su-

---

1. Reynaud's papers box 74AP22 cited in David Irving's *Churchill's War, i*, Bullsbrook, Western Australia: Veritas, p. 295.

periority. Delaying the Wehrmacht's Russian advance had helped to save both capitalist France as well as the Soviet Union.[1]

Though de Gaulle appreciated the force of Marceau Pivert's argument, he nevertheless refused to collaborate. Anxious to accrue greater backing from within existing power structures, de Gaulle understood even the remotest association with revolutionary socialists would be, from his standpoint, counter-productive. To acquire the backing from the British political establishment, as well as to have any appeal to the French upper classes, de Gaulle realised he must remain strictly inside the limits of political orthodoxy. A crucial lesson learned by the ruling classes of the various capitalist countries from the First World War was the touch paper of revolution must not be lit: short-term military gain must not be purchased at the expense of endangering long-term capitalist stability.

But there is another tune on the other side of the gramophone record. Better known than the exploits of French troops to protect the Soviet Union in 1918 are the cunning moves of the German High Command in 1917 to destroy Tsarist Russia's ability to continue the war. It resolved to allow Lenin and other Bolsheviks to travel back home from Switzerland in the famous sealed train. The German generals had their hopes fulfilled beyond their wildest expectations: from the moment he arrived at Petrograd's Finland Station, Lenin spread disaffection and the desire for peace. But if Tsarist resistance was eliminated, a different disquieting phenomenon soon replaced it. Trotsky argued that, without Lenin's physical presence in Russia – a physical presence, incidentally, that happened only by courtesy of the German High Command – a victorious October Revolution would not have happened. And within a short time this was having an adverse effect on Germany itself, both its armed forces and working class.

Hitler frequently ranted about Germany's final collapse in 1918. He attributed the defeat to subversive elements – particular agitators, Bolsheviks and Jews – spreading confusion and discontent, undermining the will to fight. Winston Churchill, too, graphically describes, in his history of the First World War, how Bolshevik propaganda spread like an epidemic among the ranks of the Wehrmacht on the Eastern front, making them no longer amenable to military discipline:

> German prisoners, liberated from Russia by the Treaty of Brest Litovsk, returned home infected by the Lenin virus. In large numbers, they refused to go again to the front.[2]

---

1. Marceau Pivert, 'An Open Letter to General de Gaulle', *New Leader*, August 1st, 1940. Also Pivert's two letters are reprinted in full in Daniel Guerin's autobiography. John McNair's unpublished autobiography, *Life Abundant*, p. 295, describes the meeting with De Gaulle. (Don Bateman Collection, Bristol University).
2. Winston Churchill, *World Crisis*, ii, p. 491. For the fact that the First World War was like a closely run race, where either side could have plucked victory, see Brian Pearce's book, *How Haig Helped Lenin* (Macmillan, 1987).

Unwittingly the various ruling classes had contributed to their undoing, the creation of convulsions of revolution that rocked Europe for years after the First World War. From that fearful experience, they learned the crucial lesson: the train to the Finland Station must never be permitted to run again. Neither of the two warring camps in the Second World War did anything that might aid or comfort revolutionary socialists. They realised the potentialities for rebellion were much greater than in the previous conflict, and therefore it would be hazardous to give them any encouragement. Reinforcing their conservative caution came the bureaucracies of social democracy and Stalinism. Together they ensured that Trotsky's prediction that the Second World War would end in a socialist revolution did not happen.

'Find out who put this in the work's suggestion box!'

The Journey to War

The British left faced the prospect of a Second World War with dark fatalism and fear. A typical reaction came in 1934 from Ellen Wilkinson and Dr Edward Conze, a refugee from fascism, then her current partner. Together they wrote a booklet, its title reveals a certain resignation, *Why War! A Handbook for Those Who Will Take Part in the Second World War*. Participants in the impending conflict were even left a few empty pages at the end, where they could scribble a few notes about the struggle. Equally certain that conflict lay ahead was F.A. Ridley. Slightly prematurely, he called his book, published in 1936, *Next Year's War*.[1]

Besides making virtually the same analysis, F.A. Ridley and Ellen Wilkinson had something else in common. When Leon Trotsky sent an American Trotskyist, Max Shachtman, as his emissary to London – his purpose being to form a revolutionary organisation in Britain – both their names were on his recruitment list. But neither joined the small group formed by Reg Groves and Harry Wicks.[2]

Yet, whatever their disagreement with Trotsky, still they remained in fundamental agreement with him on the crucial issue of war. All of them believed it remained an inherent feature of capitalism, one of its contradictions that would tend to worsen, become more destructive, over time. Unless an international socialist society were created, Trotsky forecast that the world would plunge into barbarism – what Marx in the *Communist Manifesto* had termed "the general ruin of the contending classes". The orgies of self-destruction would extinguish humanity; the planet would be left to other species, like the happy amoeba and the contented swine, sufficiently intelligent not to indulge in periodic attempts to commit collective suicide.[3]

---

1. Ellen Wilkinson and Dr Edward Conze, *Why War!*, published by the National Council of Labour Colleges, 1934, and F.A. Ridley, *Next Year's War?*, Secker & Warburg, 1936.
2. Martin Richard Upham, *The History of British Trotskyism to 1949*, pp. 32-4.
3. Leon Trotsky, *Marxism in Our Time*, Pathfinder, New York, 1969, p. 54.

Powerful forces operated in present society that were beyond control of the capitalists themselves. Businessmen wished to produce profits. None of them wished to make losses, to go bankrupt and fling themselves off tall buildings because they were completely ruined. Yet, quite independent of their volition, from time to time, their system plunges them into slumps. Similarly, wars arise not because of the wickedness of this or that individual; rather the desperate problems, created by international competition, could not be resolved in any other way.

In his little booklet, *Imperialism*, Lenin had enunciated what he saw as the basic causes of capitalist war.[1] All developed, industrialised countries were driven by the same imperatives. They needed to dominate, better still rule, places where opportunities for highly profitable investment existed. Associated with this, they needed to control sources of raw materials, necessary for their security and well-being. If plentiful supplies of cheap labour were available, then this was a further bonus. As imperial possessions were so profitable, every advanced capitalist country sought to grab them. After awhile, the problem was that, with all such territories taken, one country could only expand its empire at the expense of another. This, from Lenin's viewpoint, provided the underlying tensions which caused the First World War.

The revolutionary left argued that all these influences mentioned by Lenin continued to operate in the period before the Second World War but were augmented by other potent forces. To pull themselves out from the slump of 1929-1931, the most severe ever experienced by capitalism, the major capitalist countries turned to economic nationalism. Imperial preference, quotas, tariff barriers and barter agreements helped to provide a modicum of national security to the home-based industries. However, a semblance of economic security was gained at the cost of political insecurity. A country like Britain, safe behind the barriers it had erected, inevitably generated frustration from countries like Germany, with more dynamic economies, afraid these might explode unless new export markets were found. Slogans like 'Export or Die' (in other words, a nation's economic survival depended upon capturing foreign markets) or 'Guns or Butter?' (with its hardly hidden assumption that military means would be the ultimate arbiter) expressed the growing feeling of lethal desperation.

Trotsky saw the crisis in the following way:

> *The flagrant and ever-growing disproportion between the specific weight of France and England, not to mention Holland, Belgium and Portugal, in the world economy, and the colossal dimensions of their colonial possessions are as much the source of world conflicts and of new wars as the insatiable greed of the fascist 'aggressors'. To put it better, the two phenomena are but two sides of the same coin. The 'peaceful' British and French democracies rest on the suppression of national democratic movements of hundreds of millions in Asia and Africa for the sake of the super-profits derived from them. Conversely, Hitler*

1. Lenin, *Imperialism: The Highest Stage of Capitalism* (1916), 1944, London: Lawrence & Wishart.

and Mussolini promise to become more 'moderate' if they obtain adequate colonial territory.[1]

The Treaty of Versailles, no longer corresponding to the respective countries' economic strengths, seemed ready to buckle and break under increasing strain. How were the drastic changes to be made? The rearmament that took place in most advanced countries provided the answer.

But socialist economists pointed out rearmament posed dangerous difficulties for Britain. Margaret Laws, writing in *Controversy*, dwelt on the United Kingdom's economic decline, its lost markets. To divert production from exports to armaments would hasten this process of loss. So military strength could be gained through increasing economic weakness, a loss of markets that would never be re-conquered.[2]

Though Margaret Laws obviously was not privy to the discussions privately held by the British cabinet, her thinking – and those of other socialists – roughly corresponded with those expressed behind closed doors by many of the top

---

1. Leon Trotsky, *Writings of Leon Trotsky 1938-1939*, New York, 1969, p. 54.
2. *Controversy*, April 1939.

people. In 1931, the British cabinet had been told by the chiefs of staff that growing Japanese power threatened British possessions in the Far East: "The position is about as bad as it could be", the *Imperial Defence Review* of 1932 stated, "the whole of our territory in the Far East, as well as the coastline of India and the Dominions and our vast trade and shipping, lies open to attack".[1] A few years later it heard the same dire warnings about Italy: Britain did not possess the military might to contain any threat from Mussolini in the Mediterranean. Then, again, after Munich, Sir Alexander Cadogan told the cabinet Britain did not have the power to thwart German expansionism: "I believe that any deliberate uneconomic 'encirclement' of Germany will be futile and ruinous". He advocated "let Germany, if she can, find her 'Lebensraum' and establish herself".[2]

In view of such weakness, it might be thought government advisers might have advocated drastic rearmament. Far from it. Besides the three arms of His Majesty's Forces, Sir Thomas Inskip told ministers to protect "the fourth arm of defence" – the country's economic strength. If that were undermined, Britain would be defenceless. A sound economy underpinned everything else, and this would be jeopardised by all-out rearmament. Britain's weak economy would sink beneath the weight of military hardware.

One of the heads of British intelligence, Major Whitehead, warned ministers anyway that a "life and death struggle with Germany would bring ruination". He thought that Britain would be well-advised to try and steer Germany in an easterly direction. Hitler's *dracht nacht Osten*, his drive to the East, would eventually bring him bumping up against the Soviet Union: "From a conflict between Germany and Russia, which would probably ruin our two potential enemies in Europe, we have little to lose, and might even gain considerably".[3]

Despite not having access to secret state papers, the left sensed the big powers sparred with each other in a murky underworld of power politics. An editorial in the *New International* declared in May 1939:

> If two clever gangsters should be getting ready to fight each other, and if they wished to win public support for their respective sides, each of them could make out a plausible case. All that each would have to do, in speeches and appeals, would be to concentrate all emphasis on the crimes of the other, and let the positive argument rest on vague and noble generalities that could never be pinned down.
>
> Imperialist gangsters differ chiefly in scale from the Capones and Torrios.[4]

As more documents of the various nations become accessible, the truth of the *New International* comparison acquires still greater weight. Every government resorted to crime, deception, double-dealing. Simultaneously protestations

---

1. Chief of Staff 295, *Imperial Defence Policy*, February 23rd 1923. Cab.53/22.
2. Cadogan memo, October 14th 1938, quoted in David Dilks (ed), *Diaries of Cadogan*, pp. 116-20.
3. Cabinet Papers 316(37), 15th December 1937. Cab.24/273.
4. *New International*, May 1939.

of love and peace towards another country would be accompanied by hidden plans for war against it. This kind of conduct was akin to that practised in Renaissance Italy at the time of Machiavelli, when 'friendly' pats on the back of one diplomat by another were banned – beneath the long-flowing cloaks daggers might be concealed.

With the war approaching, Britain's policy provides a good illustration of realpolitik in operation. Seeking to lay plans for every eventuality, Chamberlain and his cabinet realised that a war with Germany was a possibility. In such circumstances, the hands of Britain and France would be strengthened if the Soviet Union could be inveigled into becoming an ally. But there were grave doubts about the Soviet Union. A backward and undeveloped country, it might quickly be crushed by an onslaught of modern armies. Moreover, Stalin had recently unleashed waves of purges. Among the many talented people he murdered were Marshal Tukhachevsky, the head of the Red Army, and many other high-ranking officers. Just as the slaying of the manager and many of the star players of a football team would place a question mark over its ability to win the world soccer cup, so doubts existed that Soviet forces, poorly equipped and poorly led, could acquit themselves well. Moreover, throughout Eastern Europe there was considerable antipathy to Russia: influence in Moscow might be won at the expense of losing much more influence elsewhere, in Poland, Rumania, etc.

Even so, the British and French governments thought no avenue must be left unexplored. So, in the summer of 1939, each government dispatched a representative for negotiations in Moscow. Dawdling along in a slow boat to Leningrad, their laid-back approach probably conveyed to the Soviet leaders the feeling that the two governments attached little importance or urgency to the mission. Once they arrived in the Kremlin, they followed normal diplomatic protocol and gave their names in full. This caused quite a stir as Britain's representative had the longest ever known surname. Soviet statesmen sat bewildered as he told them he was none other than Admiral Sir Reginald Aylmer Ranfurty Plunket-Ernle-Erle-Drax. He went on to regale them with a list of his various honours and had just reached the Order of the Bath, when one of the Russians politely inquired why the Order had gained such a peculiar title. Alas, the noble admiral did not know. On the spur of the moment he invented a story: in the Middle Ages the monarchs and their nobles enjoyed hunting. This made them dirty, and therefore afterwards they needed a wash. On hearing this explanation, the Soviet delegation fell about in laughter, presumably muttering to one another, 'It's a right one they have sent us here, tovarish'. [1]

But there were other, much more serious, reasons why the mission failed. The Soviet statesmen thought that Britain and France could not be trusted. While they would receive with alacrity Russian support if they were attacked, they would not be so enthusiastic to meet their obligations and come to Russia's aid if she were attacked. Already the Kremlin knew of manifest Anglo-French hostility dating back to the Churchill-led expeditionary force that invaded Russia

---

1. D. C. Watt, *How War Came*, London: Heinemann, 1989, pp. 452-4.

in 1919. Numerous other attempts at sabotage and spying came in later years. Virtually, as they were negotiating in 1939, a further plot was being hatched: Fitzroy Maclean, a Foreign Office agent and later, in 1941, Tory MP for Lancaster, thought the ethnic and religious unrest in Soviet Central Asia provided the opportunity to undermine Moscow control. He sought to infiltrate into the region Afghans and Iranians, for all intent and purpose looking like Soviet subjects but loyal to Britain, to fan the flames of disaffection. More recently, the newspaper *The Independent* has published details of Fitzroy Maclean's work under the headline: 'A 1939 Foreign Office Memo Saw Upheaval in Central Asia as Stalin's Achilles' Heel: British 'Plot' Aimed to Destabilise Soviets'.[1]

Another Anglo-French plan, designed to cripple the Soviet economy by bombing the Caucasus oilfields and depriving it of fuel, was also devised in 1939. The RAF aircraft doing the photographic reconnaissance of the Baku oil field encountered Russian anti-aircraft fire. These plans were frequently updated. When the Wehrmacht captured Paris in the summer of 1940, the most recently revised plans were discovered in the French Foreign Office. As the Soviet Union was then Germany's ally – the Rippentrop-Molotov pact had been signed – the Nazis passed on the plans to Moscow as a friendly gesture. Still the matter remained a serious proposition: amazingly as late as May 31st 1941, when Germany controlled the Continent and Britain stood alone, the military leaders in London still found time to contemplate bombing the Caucasus oilfields.[2]

What makes this date especially intriguing is that 31st May is only three weeks before June 22nd 1941, the day Hitler launched Barbarrosa against the Soviet Union, the biggest ever military offensive in human history. Incontestable evidence exists that Britain, for many months, had known about Hitler's plans and warned the Kremlin of the impending attack. The fascinating question remains: did some in high places want to see the invasion to be a joint German-British enterprise? As it was, German troops came close to defeating the Soviet Union. Had Britain thrown in its weight, too, it might have tipped the balance. Together, by their joint efforts, Britain and Germany may have won the vast, and largely untapped, resources of the Soviet Union, a vast new area to exploit.

Clearly, Stalin feared a combined Anglo-German onslaught might be contemplated. Maxim Litvinov, the Soviet ambassador in Washington later confided to Joseph E. Davies, an American friend of Stalinism, who had written *Mission to Moscow*, a sympathetic account of Soviet foreign policy: "All [the Russian lead-

---

1. *The Independent*, February 26th 1990; Foreign Office File N57364. Now not open to public inspection till 2015. Ironically, at the Lancaster by-election in October 1941, the Communist Party were among Fitzroy-Maclean's most vociferous supporters. They broke up an ILP election meeting and went off shouting "A vote for Brockway is a vote for Hitler".
2. Gabriel Gorodetsky, *Stafford Cripps' Mission to Moscow 1940-42*, Cambridge, 1984, pp. 24, 54, 104, 143.

ers] believed that the British fleet was steaming up the North Sea for a joint attack with Hitler on Leningrad and Kronstadt".[1]

The suspicions of Stalin must have been heightened by a mysterious event that had occurred a few days before. On May 10th 1941, Rudolf Hess, Hitler's deputy, had flown to Britain. The reasons behind this dramatic move have never been revealed. The Public Records Office still keeps some documents secret; others, according to Alan Clark, a military historian and former Minister of Defence, have been deliberately destroyed. He considers the authorities would find the revelations they contain too embarrassing: Hess, it seems, had come to negotiate peace between Britain and Germany. Whether he also wanted British participation in the attack on Russia remains unclear. That the events of May 10th 1941 and June 22nd 1941 were closely linked remained a conviction widely held. Immediately after the German offensive began a spokesman for the British Communist Party declared it was "the sequel of the secret moves which have been taking place behind the curtain of the Hess mission".[2]

Russian leaders would be mindful that only slightly more than a year before, Anglo-French and German forces came to fighting against the Soviet Union. This occurred in the final phase of the Soviet Union's war against Finland. In October 1939, Stalin attacked the Finns from a mixture of imperialist and defensive reasons. Obviously he wished to enhance the USSR's power and wealth by incorporating Finland. Yet, also, he was aware how the existing Finnish frontiers placed the Soviet Union in a dangerous military position. When he built St Petersburg, Peter the Great called it Russia's window on Europe. What he could have added was that the Finnish-owned Aaland islands, strategically situated in the Baltic, constituted the shutters that at any time could be used to block off the window. Moreover, the Russo-Finnish frontiers then ran precariously near to Leningrad, the country's second city, putting it within easy shelling distance. This was made more menacing because many of the big powers, potential enemies of the Soviet Union, had for years helped to build up Finland militarily. And this is what happened during the winter war: supplies came from Britain, France and Germany. As Finland's position deteriorated, these countries decided to stiffen resistance by sending their own troops to fight alongside the Finns. On February 5th 1940, the Allied Supreme War Council decided to dispatch six British divisions and 50,000 French troops. Three hundred British volunteers, presumably the precursors of the present-day SAS, had already arrived in Helsinki. The prospect of Anglo-French troops fighting alongside German ones was only thwarted because Finland sued for peace on February 29th 1940.[3]

But, if it was not inconceivable to find British and French troops fighting alongside their German counterparts, then there is another scenario that has been discreetly forgotten: British-French hostility towards the United States

1. J. E. Davies papers, Box 11 (Library of Congress). Also Lord Halifax papers A.7.8.9, diary December 11th 1941.
2. *Daily Express*, 23rd June 1941.
3. Neville Chamberlain, House of Commons, 19th March 1940.

Though it may seem weird today, American military manoeuvres in the 1920s were held on the supposition that America was being invaded by British troops stationed in Canada! In 1929, the US government drew up top secret plans for war with Britain, aimed at driving the British from both North and South America. This fear of an Anglo-American war may have receded slightly in the 1930s. Even so, big sources of tension still remained, particularly in the Pacific and Latin America. On March 17th 1939, two events happened: first, German troops marched into Prague; and, second, this violation of the recently-signed Munich agreement did not stop the Dusseldorf accords between the Federation of British Industry and Reichsgruppe Industrie, its German equivalent, being signed. Their objective was to strengthen Anglo-German economic co-operation, thereby enhancing their mutually competitive position throughout the world.

Both the prime minister, Neville Chamberlain, and Oliver Stanley, president of the Board of Trade, publicly welcomed the agreement. In May 1939, they agreed to the Bank of International Settlement sending $25 million worth of Czech gold from London to Berlin. Two British government advisers, Robert Hudson and Sir Horace Wilson, negotiated with their Nazi counterparts the possibility of a $5,000 million loan to the Third Reich. The British ambassador to Germany, Sir Nevile Henderson, stated these were all signs of Britain offering the hand of friendship to Germany.[1]

As the British left recognised, the Dusseldorf accords and other measures were designed primarily as an anti-American move. In *Labour Monthly* of May 1939, John Strachey's article, commenting on the Dusseldorf accords, was headed 'Mr Chamberlain's Anti-Americanism'. Both big business and the Tory government hoped Anglo-German cooperation would halt the United States economic advance in Latin America. Together, they thought, they might be able to stop the erosion of British influence there while simultaneously helping Germany successfully to counter the growing Yankee dominance of the continent. United they would stand; divided they would fall to the Dollar.

Old habits die hard; so do old antipathies. Even when, in the 1940s, Britain and Germany had been foes for years, a lot of influential Americans found it difficult to recognise the changed relationship. In his history of the OSS, the forerunner of the CIA, Professor R. Harris Smith plainly admitted: "Many OSS men began to operate on the general principle that the British are just as much the enemy as the Germans. They believed that London's secret services were more concerned with expanding England's empire than with defeating the enemy".[2]

Yet, US foreign policy appears to have been equally prefaced by considerations of self-interest. Up to Munich in 1938, it strived to maintain peace. Soviet historians suggest this was done because any war would be of short dura-

---

1. D. F. Fleming, *Cold War*, i, p. 92.

2. Peter Tompkins, *Italy Betrayed*, New York: Simon & Schuster, p. 253, and R. Harris Smith, *OSS: The Secret History of America's First Central Intelligence Agency*, University of California, 1972, p. 34.

'Look! There's your enemy!'

tion, affording the United States with little opportunity to expand exports to either belligerents. However, as it became likely any conflict would be both prolonged and of great severity, American foreign policy changed. It threatened that, unless Britain and France stood up to German expansionism, their supplies of vital raw materials would be cut off. Joseph P. Kennedy, American ambassador in London, said that:

> neither the French nor the British would have made Poland a cause of war if it had not been for the constant needling from Washington... In the summer of 1939, the President kept telling him (Kennedy) to put some iron up Chamberlain's backside![1]

But there was more than a hint of American double-dealing and Double-crossing. In early October 1939, President Roosevelt sent a personal envoy to Berlin. He was William Rhodes Davis, an influential oil tycoon. In the discussion, Davis assured the Nazi leaders that Roosevelt's main strategic concern was to destroy Britain's position in world markets. The President wished to know Germany's terms for a peace settlement. He would then bring pressure for British and French compliance. Were they to fail to do so, then the United

---

1. Charles C. Tansill, *Back Door to War: The Roosevelt Foreign Policy*, Chicago, 1952, p. 555

States would supply Germany with goods and war material "convoyed to Germany under the protection of the American armed forces".[1]

Amid the myriad of plots and counter-plots, deceptions and subterfuges, indulged in by the major powers, it may appear difficult to disentangle how any country determined its foreign policy. Doubtless, a considerable amount of uncertainty prevailed, with contingency plans for fighting a large number of possible enemies. Equally, the allies were also as numerous. In these circumstances, it seems hardly surprising that Trotsky, a perceptive observer of international affairs in 1938 predicted a war would occur but was unwilling to forecast the line-up of protagonists.

Nevertheless, a useful clue as to what were the crucial domestic influences that helped to determine British foreign policy may come unwittingly from a well-known remark of Chamberlain, made soon after Munich. He described Czechoslovakia as a far away country about which most people knew nothing. This was probably true of 80% of the British population. In those days communications were not so highly developed as today; few Britons would have ever met a Czech; most would not be unduly perturbed about its fate. But who would be concerned? Certainly, businessmen, financiers and traders who had economic links with Czechoslovakia would. They would be concerned with whether they could continue, perhaps expand, their operations; of the social climate of a country in which they functioned; and of whether the political structure was congenial and provided security. So it would be these capitalist interests that would have a definite opinion of what should be done, whether there should be peace or war. The input to the decision-making process of the working-class, usually limited on home affairs, would be much more limited on foreign issues.

Of course, whatever decision was taken would have its impact elsewhere. Britain's failure to resist German encroachments in Czechoslovakia sent a shiver of insecurity to those with economic ties in the Balkans and even into the Middle East. Britain's decision later, however, to go to war over the invasion of Poland would have exactly the opposite repercussions. But with the country's resources committed to war against Germany, the already inadequate cover provided elsewhere would be weakened still further. While Britain was preoccupied, America, Italy, Japan and Russia would feel under less restraint to respect British interests. (By British interests, of course, we always mean British Capitalist interests; workers would merely act as spectators.)

Consequently diplomacy is like an iceberg, with seven-eighths hidden from view. Most of the lobbying and negotiating is conducted informally in secret. It remains, nevertheless, effective. The human moneybags get their way silently, without the public even hearing the clink of coinage. Similarly, with peace discussions: in neutral countries – say, Sweden or Spain – businessmen from many nations use the same restaurants. Friend and foe may meet over a drink and exchange views. In such circumstances, the respective embassies can ask its

---

1. David Irving, *The War Path: Hitler's Germany 1933-1939*, London: Macmillan, 1978, p. 32.

businessmen to float a proposal, act as a sounding board. Should a proposal appear acceptable, then it can be taken up later through official channels. Should it prove an embarrassment, then it can simply be disowned.

In the Second World War, the influence of the wealthy in the decision-making process was strong in every country. As we have seen, the oil magnate, William Rhodes Davis, was Roosevelt's emissary at the beginning of the conflict. In the final phase, Myrom Taylor, the tough leader of the American steel bosses, helped to secure a peace favourable to US interests. Then, between big business and the intelligence services, a lot of intermeshing occurred. One of America's wealthiest men, Andrew Mellon's son Paul was at OSS's Special Operations Branch in London. His sister Ailsa, one of the world's richest women, was married to David Bruce, head of OSS operations in London. He was son of a senator and was a millionaire in his own right. Other Mellons and Mellon in-laws held OSS positions in Madrid, Geneva and Paris. And so one could go on.[1]

Of course, in Britain Chamberlain's government represented capitalist interests. Where divisions existed on a foreign policy issue, then usually there were no inhibitions about battling for one's corner. In her famous book about Jarrow, Ellen Wilkinson does not suggest it met a natural death. Her title was not *The Town that Died* but *The Town that was Murdered* – and murder involves a deliberate, conscious act. She explained how a British and German shipbuilders' cartel sought to restrict production so profits could be increased. The slaughter of Jarrow shipyard was the consequence. Because of the mutually advantageous arrangements, many industrialists did not want Britain to go to war with Germany. Six of their representatives conducted secret negotiations in an attempt

---

1. Harris Smith, op. cit., pp. 15-6.

to avert the conflict. Those involved in this move were: Sir Charles Maclaren, of Thomas Brown (shipbuilder), S.W. Dawson of Thomas Forth (steel manufacturer), Sir Robert Renwick of London Electrical Supply, Brian S. Mountain of Eagle Star (investment and insurance), Frederick Spicer of Thomas Brown and T. Mensforth of Hotpoint (electrical manufacturer). At the Nuremburg war crimes trial in 1946, Herman Goering commended their efforts to secure peace.

But the supreme Nazi accolade went to Lord Londonderry, a one-time treasurer of the Conservative Party and County Durham's biggest coal owner. In 1938, Penguin published his book, *Ourselves and Germany*. The blurb stated:

> It is the clearest exposition so far of the policy of rapprochement with Nazi Germany and for a more sympathetic Herr Hitler's point of view. Few men have played such an important part in our diplomatic relations with Germany as Lord Londonderry. During his frequent visits abroad he spent considerable time with Hitler, Goering, Neurath and Ribbentrop.

As if to underline the prevailing spirit of goodwill, the book finishes with letters commending the work from Field-Marshal Goering, Franz von Papen, Joachim Stresemann and the Bishop of Durham. However, the first letter, saying how much he has enjoyed reading the book and appreciates His Lordship's efforts to promote Anglo–German understanding, ends:

> With my best wishes to Lady Londonderry and with friendly greetings, Yours cordially, Adolf Hitler.

In the circumstances, was it surprising that an Anglo-German coal agreement was signed in January 1939 – in other words, two months before the Dusseldorf accords.

Besides those wanting Anglo-German cooperation (because when two are shaking the trees' branches more plums are likely to drop off than if one was doing it alone) there was another group with slightly different interests who wanted to promote better relations between Britain and Germany. A multinational firm like Unilever felt war would disrupt its business. This probably prompted four of its directors to sit on the governing body of the Anglo-German Friendship Society.

Though powerful influences were operating to stop amity with Germany, government ministers had to decide from where weak and ailing Britain was menaced the most. To put all its efforts into a life-and-death struggle with country A necessarily meant that the already inadequate resources to protect British interests against countries B, C and D would be further depleted. Consequently, war against one nation, even if it ended in victory, would mean silently enduring losses inflicted by others. A balance sheet has two sides. Arriving at a decision about who to fight involved an agonising process. It was only resolved in August 1939 by the Molotov-Ribbentrop pact. The agreement reached between Germany and the Soviet Union represented a threat to British interests throughout the world, a threat that far exceeded the gains that British firms might hope to accrue from possible Anglo-German cooperation.

For centuries, Britain had sought to maintain a balance of power in Europe, stopping any state from achieving dominance of the continent Clearly, the combined strength of Germany and Russia would make them supreme. Then together, controlling a vast land-mass, stretching from Europe to the Middle East and the Pacific Ocean, virtually the entire British Empire would be under threat And, finally, against the two-headed monster, even the British Isles themselves would be imperilled. So reluctantly on September 3rd 1939, Neville Chamberlain, the British prime minister, declared war.

Never was so much, owed by so few to so many

Betrayal on the Left

Before 1939, the Marxist left found itself in a position akin to that of Cassandra, the figure in Classical mythology who could foretell impending disasters but could do nothing to avert them. Victor Serge, the famous writer and revolutionary, called this period 'the midnight of the century': the forces of evil triumphed while the forces of good suffered defeat and demoralisation. The defeat of the General Strike in 1926 dealt a savage blow against organised labour. Not only did it leave many miners unemployed, but militants from other occupations joined the dole queues. The following year the government introduced fresh anti-union legislation. Simultaneously, Chiang Kai-Shek drowned the Chinese Revolution in blood and with it any prospect of saving Russia through the achievement of socialism elsewhere. In 1928, exploiting the threats, both internal and external, Stalin swept away all the gains of the October Revolution and imposed his cruel dictatorship on the Soviet Union. Then came the Wall Street crash, sending shock waves throughout the world economy and causing mass unemployment in every industrialised country. Unable to meet the challenge in a socialist way the Labour government toppled when the cabinet split over whether to make swingeing public expenditure cuts. By the autumn or 1931, Ramsay MacDonald and some of the other Labour leaders belonged to a Tory-dominated National government that had routed the Party, reducing its representation in the Commons from 287 MPs to a mere 46. In 1933 Hitler came to power in Germany Two years later fascist Italy invaded Abyssinia and used poison gas on the natives. Then came the Spanish civil war, the overthrowal of parliamentary democracy throughout the entire Iberian peninsular, followed by Nazi expansion into Austria and Czechoslovakia.

There is a saying 'Nothing succeeds like success'. In his *Maxims for Revolutionists*, Bernard Shaw substituted the word 'excess'! But, whichever is correct, one thing remains certain; nothing fails as abysmally as failure. The hammer blows hit workers so hard, so relentlessly, it robbed them of self-confidence and self-reliance. Instead of developing their own powers, seeing a new society could only arise through class struggle, they relapsed into disgruntled apathy.

Throughout the Thirties, most people felt, to use Shakespeare's phrase, "calm'd, cribbed, confined, condemned to saucy doubts and ears". Admittedly, they might have the benefits of newfangled inventions – the radio and, for a very few, the motorcar – but at a more fundamental level they were being deprived of their humanity. Less and less did they have control of their own lives. Most stood as passive spectators, convinced they could not influence events. Some of the courageous few resorted to acts of individual defiance.

In the summer of 1939, a young Cambridge undergraduate went to the cinema. He sat quietly through the feature film. When a short was screened, urging young men to join the army, he took out a bugle and blew it until he was eventually ejected. The young man was Alex Comfort, destined to become a distinguished scientist, a pioneer of gerontology, the process of ageing, though he became better known for his manuals on sex. Actually, he would prefer to be known as a writer and for his political views.[1] In 1939, he thought the only way a holocaust could be stopped was by acts of mass defiance. If mankind wanted to save itself, it must answer the recruiting sergeant's order not with a salute but a sock to the jaw. In a poem for his son, he gave the warning:

> Remember when you hear them beginning to say Freedom
> Look carefully – see who it is they want you to butcher.

Comfort emphasised that the carnage depended upon working people. Without their acquiescence, it could not happen. His poem ends:

> So that because the woodcutter disobeyed
> they will not burn her to-day or any day
>
> So that for lack of a joiner's obedience
> the crucifixion will not now take place
>
> So that when they come to sell you their bloody corruption
> you will gather the spit of your chest
> And plant it in their faces.[2]

Though causing irritation, perhaps temporary difficulties, individual acts of disobedience, like those of Alex Comfort, do not seriously threaten the state authorities. It is not enough to get an individual joiner or woodcutter to disobey; what is required is to get their defiance *en masse* – not as a person but as class action.

Insofar as an awareness of the need to do something existed, workers tended to look to saviours from on high for their salvation. The two candidates that

---

1. A collection of Alex Comfort's writings, *Against Power and Death*, ed. David Goodway, was published by Freedom Press, 1994.
2. Alex Comfort's poem, 'The Song of Lazarus', ultimately appeared in *New Road* 1945, London, pp. 11-20.

came readily to hand were the Labour and Communist parties. Let us consider them in turn.

Well before 1939, Labour had become thoroughly integrated into the capitalist system. Its leaders remained eager to clamber up into its higher echelons of the ruling class. The pomp and ceremony of state occasions, the glamour of high society, the prestige flowing from acquiring honours – all aspects of the good life proved irresistible to the Snowdens, Thomases and Co. Ramsay MacDonald took 'the aristocratic embrace' quite literally. A year after the Foreign Office, considering him such a valuable governmental asset, had paid out the then not inconsiderable sum of £10,000 in hush money to prevent the scandal of his sexual entanglement with a French lady from becoming public knowledge, MacDonald turned his attentions to the wife of County Durham's biggest coal owner. The fact that he had just been elected at the 1929 general election as Member of Parliament for the Seaham constituency and that the miners in the constituency had downed tools because Lord Londonderry planned to worsen still further their pay and conditions did not affect his amatory adventure. His love letters to Lady Londonderry began "Dear Circe" (after the Greek goddess who set men's hearts aflame) and ended "Hamish the Hunter".[1] The great romance became a popular topic for parliamentary gossip. At one meeting, Jimmy Maxton, the Clydeside rebel, jocularly proposed the Labour Party should change its anthem from 'The Red Flag' to 'The Londonderry Air'.[2]

At first glance, it may appear merely a trivial personal matter. But personal conduct and political principles remain closely intertwined. This particularly applies in periods that, to use Thomas Paine's phrase, try men's souls. In 1917 the Bolsheviks faced many formidable obstacles. There was one problem, however, that they did not encounter: when storming the Winter Palace in St Petersburg, they did not have to worry about whether members of the Communist Party central committee would be inside, cavorting at a social function of Tsarist high society. Nor was there any possibility that they would discover Lenin in a compromising amorous liaison with some aristocratic Russian lady. To suggest that such was even a remote possibility would have been equally repugnant to both Bolsheviks and the Romanovs. Similarly in the English civil war, the period of revolutionary change in Britain, a stark divide prevailed: the forces of king and Parliament were quite distinct. They represented two conflicting sets of political principles, contrasting social values and markedly different ways of life. Nobody had the least difficulty in distinguishing a follower of Cromwell from a follower of the crown – the dress of a Roundhead from that of a Cavalier.

In the 1930s, a number of consequences flowed from Labour's incorporation. Striving to be accepted as the alternative government in waiting, a party that could be entrusted to protect carefully the existing system, it needed an image

---

1. David Marquand, *Ramsay MacDonald* (London, 1977), pp. 495-5, 687-92, 783. For the French scandal, see Richard Deacon, *C: A Biography of Sir Richard Oldfield, Head of MI6* (London, 1985), p. 185.
2. Claud Cockburn, *Crossing the Line*, London, 1958, p. 45.

of respectability. This meant Labour could not back campaigns against poor housing, poverty and unemployment that might even remotely destabilise capitalism, generating anger against these evils. Far from campaigning alongside workers in their struggles for higher wages and better conditions, the Labour leaders needed to show themselves capable of restoring class peace. In such circumstances, Labour could not support the hunger marches, led by communists like Wal Hannington and Harry McShane. But the Labour bosses indicated they were not even prepared to back ultra-respectable campaigns. At the Edinburgh Labour Party conference in 1937, Lucy Middleton, for the National Executive Committee, denounced the Jarrow crusade, a cry for work that had the support of all sections of Jarrow society, including the local Tories.[1] To have clapped Jarrow would have created an ugly precedent: millions of others, angered that they had been denied a job, would look to the Labour Party for help.

A further disincentive for the Labour leaders, anxious to court acceptance by the system, not agitation by the masses, was that the Jarrow crusade had received backing from the communist press. The fact that only one of the 200 original marchers was a communist, and he was promptly sent home once his political allegiance was discovered, was immaterial. It still left the Labour Party with an odour of disreputability.

Obviously anything that smacked of communism needed to be shunned. Labour leaders did not want there to be the slightest suspicion that they were not truly British but agents of a foreign power. Labour Party members were forbidden from participating in anti-fascist campaigns where communists were involved; a prohibition that even affected a young Hugh Gaitskell, then the prospective candidate for Gravesend but later to be a right-wing leader of the Party. Likewise, because Hitler had so inconsiderately persecuted German communists as well as Jews, socialists and others, the Labour Party placed The British Committee for the Relief of the Victims of German Fascism on its list of proscribed organisations. This meant that the Committee's president, Professor Albert Einstein, would not be permitted to join the Labour Party even if he had been so ill-advised as to want to do so.

Intolerance stalked Labour's higher reaches. In 1937, it banned the Socialist League, led by Sir Stafford Cripps, a body that strived to abolish capitalism through parliamentary means. Two years later it decided to disband its youth section–the Labour League of Youth–because it was too left. At the same annual conference, it resolved to deprive Sir Stafford Cripps and his main supporters of their party membership. Cripps' 'crime', hardly heinous, hardly intrinsically left, was to propose the Party seek an electoral arrangement. With a general election fast approaching–the previous one had been in 1935–he wanted Labour, Liberal and Conservative candidates opposed to Chamberlain's foreign policy to make an electoral alliance. Behind this notion, essentially a Communist notion of a popular front but minus the relatively insignificant Communist Party, lay the calculations of the findings of the most recent opinion poll: at a general election 50% of the electorate would vote Tory, 42% for

1. Labour Party annual conference report 1937, p. 158.

the Labour and Liberal opposition.[1] Even with an electoral arrangement, the opposition would have immense difficulty to oust Chamberlain.

The response of somebody truly left would have been to have campaigned to involve in political protest those who had suffered – the poor, the unemployed and others – whose voice had not been heard. But Cripps' position was that, rather than to try to mobilise working-class anger, not tapped by the Labour Party, he would look to the likes of Winston Churchill to be saviours. When the Labour Party National Executive Committee organisational sub-committee met to conduct its preliminary investigation into Cripps' position, Sir Stafford informed them he would be unable to attend. One of the best paid barristers in Britain, Sir Stafford gave priority to the legal demands of his client – the Midland Bank – over those of attending the Labour Party NEC's disciplinary hearing, to answer the charges against him. Presumably, somewhat annoyed, the NEC of the Labour Party resolved to deprive him of party membership. A clutch of other dissenters, including Aneurin Bevan, were also expelled. Bevan considered the expulsions signalled the end of internal party democracy, the right of members to campaign for views contrary to those of the party leadership. He added, "Socialist propaganda has practically ceased. Socialist organisation is in cold storage".[2]

Actually, the Labour leaders simultaneously mixed tolerance with intolerance: on to those within its own ranks, wanting to anchor the Party to positions that they found unacceptable, like Cripps' line which was more favourable to the Soviet Union than to Nazi Germany, the iron fist of discipline came crashing down. However, to the Conservative government, a much more favourable, tolerant attitude prevailed. They were regarded not as deadly enemies but as essentially good chaps. All the Labour leaders desired was a little space in which to manoeuvre, where they could put forward their minor disagreements with the Conservatives.

On June 27th 1939, an official Labour delegation – Dalton, Citrine and Morrison – saw the prime minister. In the discussion, Chamberlain offered to give Labour politicians posts in his government. The Labour leaders, after much thought, rejected Chamberlain's offer. Presumably, they felt they would only be given the most unpopular posts, the ones that would not enhance their electoral standing in the election at most a few months away. Far better play safe: let the Tories take the fateful decision, declaring war on Germany; for Labour to be directly involved might enhance the unrest of its own rank and file.

Even so, that Chamberlain could make this kind of offer and for the Labour leadership to spend a lengthy period pondering on whether to accept it or not shows a mutual recognition existed that fundamentally both parties accepted the same political principles. For years Labour had embraced the essentials of Tory politics, not merely on domestic but equally on foreign issues. It should be remembered that, despite its economic decline, Britain still possessed the world's biggest empire, a source of immense wealth for a privileged few in the

---

1. Gallup poll results appeared in the *News Chronicle*, February 11th 1939.
2. *Tribune*, July 26th 1939.

mother country. Other countries, covetous of Britain's colonies and conscious that economic decline made protecting them an increasingly arduous task, were tempted to seek to seize them by force.

When in 1934 Ellen Wilkinson and Dr Edward Conze wrote their booklet, *Why War?*, they argued that the Labour Party would do nothing to prevent the imperialist war because Labour backed the Empire with the same alacrity as the Tories. It readily embraced the use of the same means, the same aims, they pointed out, as the Tories – to maintain the British Raj:

> *The colonial native can hardly notice the difference between a Labour or a Conservative government. Mr William Leach, the Labour under secretary for the Colonies in 1923-4, explained the essential humanity of bombing Iraqi villages in terms which were certainly not bettered by Sir John Simon's passionate plea for the continuance of this mercy on the North Western Frontier.*[1]

The second Labour government (1929-1931), as well as consistently continuing the same policy of bombing native villages, underlined its determination to preserve the British Raj by answering the Indian campaign for national independence with beatings, shootings and wholesale arrests on an unprecedented scale.

Ramsay MacDonald's desertion of the Labour Party did not make a whit of difference. Along with ex-Labour leaders and their new Tory cabinet companions, as prime minister of the National government, MacDonald continued to bomb civilians in India and the Middle East. In 1933, he sent his friend Lord Londonderry as Britain's representative to the World Disarmament Conference. Like other countries, Britain expressed its devotion to the cause of peace. But then his Lordship went on to suggest disarmament should start with those weapons that would not disadvantage the United Kingdom; much later, if ever, getting on to those that effected national security. Lord Londonderry told delegates Britain vitally needed bombing aircraft. It was an essential weapon in dealing with 'the dissident tribesmen on the North West Indian frontier'. (For this read: the grandfathers of those who, a couple of generations later, were to be called 'Afghan freedom fighters'.) Though the World Disarmament Conference would probably have failed anyway, by trumpeting the cause of the bomber, Britain modestly could claim to have played its part in achieving the conference's collapse, a result that laid the basis for the Luftwaffe blitz of Britain in 1940-1941.[2]

As John Scanlon, a Clydeside worker, sarcastically explained in his book, *Very Foreign Affairs*:

> *Lord Londonderry dared not abolish the bombing plane without breaking the doctrine established by his predecessors at the Air Ministry – Lord Thomson and Mr William Leach. Far from being a dangerous armament, in their view the bombing plane was not a weapon of offence. Strictly speaking, it should not*

1. Ellen Wilkinson and Edward Conze, *Why War!* , London 1934, p. 42.
2. Malcolm Muggeridge, *The Thirties in Great Britain*, London, 1940, p. 136

be included in the list of armaments but should be charged up to the Red Cross account.[1]

And so it continued. In 1938, Emrys Hughes castigated the Parliamentary Labour Party because, instead of censoring the Government for leaving the unemployed with insufficient money to properly feed their families and keep them warm in the wintry cold, it had criticised Chamberlain for his failure to accumulate more weapons of mass destruction more quickly:

> *We have already had the spectacle of Dr Hugh Dalton, a Labour front-bencher, moving on behalf of the Labour Party a motion criticising the Government because of the slow production of bombing planes. And when Dr Dalton sat down, Mr Winston Churchill rose to compliment him warmly on his speech.[2]*

The aircraft remained a symbol of modern scientific technology, the quintessential representation of imperialist power. Gunboat diplomacy of Victorian times was replaced by 20th century bomber diplomacy. Suddenly an aeroplane, appearing in the sky as if from nowhere, could wreak havoc, terrorising unsuspecting native villages with its bombs and bullets. From the standpoint of the colonial power, airborne intervention had a number of distinct advantages. Millions of people in Africa and Asia could be cowered into submission by a few daring young men in their flying machines. The whole thing was comparatively cheap both in men and money, as both politicians and military historians recognised: at little danger to themselves, a few airmen could preserve colonial rule over vast areas.[3]

The mass of Labour supporters did not understand this trigonometry of colonial oppression. All they wanted, nay, fervently desired, was peace, and naively they believed that their leaders held the same opinion. As the moment of truth – or, rather, the moment of war – approached, it became clear the desires of the audience and of their spokesmen, who combined public professions of desiring peace with basically backing the Tories, were wildly at odds.

The pervasive unease of Labour's leaders and their followers was vividly captured by that organ of big business, *The Economist*. It described Labour's internal crisis as follows:

> *The paradox of the present situation in this country is that it is not Mr Chamberlain but Mr Attlee who is, at the moment, exerting himself to prevent the formation of an opposition that might have a chance of turning the present government out. So long as this situation remains unchanged, the Labour Party's fulminations against Mr Chamberlain will remain unconvincing. In Spain, they used to practice 'rotavism' by which two nominally contending political parties took offices and resigned, turn and turn about, on an agreed timetable. Mr Attlee's tacit understanding with Mr Chamberlain is still more quaint.*

---

1. John Scanlon, *Very Foreign Affairs*, London, 1938, p. 242.
2. *Forward*, March 22nd 1938.
3. For a good account of the military role of bombing aircraft, see V. G. Kiernan, *European Empires from Conquest to Collapse, 1815-1960*, London, 1982, pp. 194-7.

> *He will see to it that Mr Chamberlain and his friends shall be His Majesty's*
> *eternal Government so long as Mr Attlee and his friends can be His Majesty's*
> *eternal Opposition.*[1]

In the immediate period before the outbreak of war, Attlee was a political
spectator, a consequence of illness caused by prostate trouble. Arthur Greenwood, deputising for him as Labour leader, made a staunchly pro-war speech.
To cheers and shouts of "Speak for England, Arthur", from Leo Amery and
other MPs on the Tory right, he made it clear that the Labour Party believed
Britain should go to war over Poland irrespective of the consequences. The
fact that Marshal Pilsudski's regime in Poland was also a brutal dictatorship
like Hitler's in Germany, as well as oppressing national minorities and crushing
working-class organisations, seemed to him to matter not one jot. At the end
of the Commons' debate, Greenwood pounded up the stairs after Chamberlain.
"You could not see your supporters", he told the prime minister. "I could. I
know their feeling is mine".[2]

Among the Labour leadership, none was more jingoistic than Hugh Dalton.
He came from a high Church and high Tory background. His father had been
Canon of St George's chapel, Windsor, and for fourteen years had been tutor
to the sons of Edward VII. Apparently, he joined the Labour Party out of
pique, after not being allowed to join an elite society at Eton. As historian T.D.
Burridge says, he "presented almost the caricature of the dyed-in-the-wool
Tory background from which he sprung". Expressing a hatred of all things
German, including the German working class, Dalton combined his racism with
a belief that Britain should go to war regardless of what France decided to do.[3]

This approach evoked criticism from persons who could not be considered
left-wingers. For example, Bernard Shaw objected to the racism and simplistic
explanation that, rather than seeing that the causes of war lay in the system,
sought to blame everything on all things German:

> *So far the Parliamentary Labour Party and its newspaper, the* Daily Herald,
> *have gone as wrong as possible on the war. No Primrose League gathering could*
> *outdo them. Far from being a party of the left, they have clean gone over to the*
> *right of Mr Chamberlain.*[4]

It is interesting to compare the Labour Party's attitude to the First World
War with that to the Second. In 1914, Keir Hardie, Labour's representative at
the Socialist International, firmly and tenaciously tried to prevent war. Though
Keir Hardie could be termed a pacifist internationalist, not a revolutionary
socialist, he staunchly believed people throughout the world had nothing to
gain from mass slaughter. He staunchly maintained this stand though it left

---

1. *The Economist*, March 4th 1939.
2. Kenneth Harris, *Attlee*, London, 1982, pp. 163-4; D. C. Watt, *How War Came*,
London, 1989, pp. 579-580; Ben Pimlott, *Labour and the Left in the 1930s*, Cambridge,
1977, pp. 183-4.
3. T. D. Burridge, *British Labour and Hitler's War*, London, 1976, p. 29.
4. *New Leader*, October 13 1939. The Primrose League was a right-wing Tory society.

him increasingly out of step with the majority of the Labour leaders. Yet, even when they submitted to war fever, Keir Hardie never turned into a jingo. What a marked contrast with the position on the eve of the Second World War, when the Labour Party had integrated itself thoroughly within the existing system. The Labour leaders of 1939 stood out as Britain's most outspoken warmongers. 'abc'

The second saviour from on high – a political force that might avert world conflict – was the Soviet Union, with the British Communist Party basking in its reflected glory. In 1917, a workers' revolution had occurred; many oppressed people throughout the world greeted the creation of a system that opposed exploitation. Towards Russia, a tremendous goodwill existed among revolutionary socialists.

But this overlooked the emergence of a number of fatal flaws. First, because the Soviet Union was an extremely backward nation, it did not possess the essentials of life necessary to create a socialist society. For example, as late as 1935, official Soviet statistics show the production of shoes was insufficient to provide citizens with one pair of shoes a year each. In other words, the primitive level of productive forces meant – to quote Marx's inelegant phrase – "the old crap" returning. There had to be those with shoes and those without shoes: a class division between haves and have-nots. In an economically backward and beleaguered Soviet Union, who determined the division of wealth? Obviously the few who could read and write – the bureaucracy – saw to their own requirements first. Equally, the military chiefs, the officer caste of the Red Army, which had repelled nineteen marauding armies of intervention, did not lack shoes. A privileged class, divorced and hostile proletariat, seized the state apparatus under Stalin, using it for the furtherance of its own interests. Far from striving for socialism throughout the world, the Kremlin's bosses simply sought to promote its own exploitative aims – in behaviour no different to any other ruling class.

Most class-conscious workers in Britain remained oblivious of these Russian developments. Dismissing the one-man dictatorship and purges as capitalist propaganda, they focussed on the positive features – rapid industrial growth, with the five-year plan accomplished in four years, the establishment of full employment and steadily rising living standards. These seemed in stark contrast to what was happening in Britain, with its industrial graveyards and millions of unemployed. The Soviet Union appeared a shining star of socialist light, made all the brighter because of the depressed and depressive conditions in this country.

The British Communist Party wallowed in the reflected glory emanating from the East. While Communist Party headquarters did receive Moscow gold, a much more potent reason for the Communist Party's growth in the 1930s was the fund of goodwill a lot of class-conscious workers felt for the Soviet Union. Yet, the price paid was slavish obedience, the acceptance of every command coming from the Kremlin. These could be unintelligible or perhaps even obscene: Claud Cockburn recounts an occasion on which Moscow stated that 'the lower organs of the party in Britain must make still greater efforts to penetrate the backward parts of the proletariat'.[1]

Other Comintern edicts called for the abandonment of personal integrity. For example, Robin Page Arnot, one of the Communist Party's leading historians, wrote two histories of the Russian Revolution. The first, written before Stalinisation, stated quite truthfully that Lenin and Trotsky led the Soviets to power. By the time the second appeared, Stalin's one-man dictatorship had emerged. Consequently, history was re-written: Page Arnot described how this 'great' Georgian, Stalin, stood alongside Lenin, receiving the victors' accolade. Trotsky had been relegated to the political underworld, where he lurked as a counter-revolutionary devil. The same approach operated when the liberal *News Chronicle* sought to serialise John Reed's book, *Ten Days that Shook the World*. The Communist Party held the copyright, and stated permission would only be granted if all references to Trotsky were expunged. To that, the *News Chronicle* responded it would be like publishing Hamlet minus the Prince of Denmark and withdrew its request.[2]

The bizarre treatment of George Padmore, an immensely talented West Indian Marxist, illustrates that a sinister subscript lay beneath the desire to be 'economical with the truth'. He wrote a first-rate scholarly book on '*British Capitalism in Africa*'. The independent, left wing publisher Martin Lawrence signed a contract with him to get it out. Before this could occur, however, two things happened: first, the firm of Martin Lawrence was taken over and became part of Lawrence & Wishart, a concern completely subservient to the Communist Party; and second, the Soviet Union and France had signed a friendship pact, making France overnight a progressive and peace loving country. Hence the British Communist Party demanded that Padmore cut out every uncomplimentary reference to France from his book. When Padmore refused saying that, if anything, the conditions of the natives in French colonies had worsened in recent years, it put the Communist Party apparatchiks in a deep dilemma – the contract had been signed and had to be honoured; the book took a line contrary to party policy.

The Stalinist bosses of the British Party sought to resolve their difficulties in a manner unique in the annals of publishing: Lawrence & Wishart produced Padmore's book – and then issued publicity to discourage people from buying it! An irate George Padmore was interviewed by Reginald Reynolds, who published his article in *Controversy* under the heading 'A Publisher's Acrobatics'.[3]

Other independent left journals took up the issue, too. The conclusion was there to be drawn: the Communist Party and its fellow travelling organisations did not determine its policy on the basis of the exploitation and suffering of a working class – rather it was on whether the ruling class would play kissing-the-ring with the rulers of the Kremlin. It was the attitude towards the

1. Claud Cockburn, op cit., p. 55.
2. Stalinist falsification was repeatedly exposed in journals such as *Controversy*, *Forward*, *New Leader* as well as in Trotskyist magazines.
3. *Controversy*, July 1937.

Russian state that remained the crucial determinant. This was spectacularly shown in 1941: on June 21st at 5.29 am, as they slept in their beds, the Second World War was reactionary – it needed to be opposed – but at 6.30 am, when the Wehrmacht launched its invasion of the Soviet Union, all suddenly changed: policies of the British government which previously had been attacked had now to be defended, strikes that had been supported now had to be broken.

Yet, this did not begin in 1941. Significantly, Roger Hollis, head of MI5, in a lecture to British intelligence and police officers, said he thought the CPGB had jettisoned all pretensions to being a revolutionary organisation in 1935, when it embraced the Popular Front.[1] In Britain it meant the Communist Party seeking to build an alliance with individuals from other parties – Labour, Liberal and Tory – who embraced the proposition that Germany constituted the main threat to British interests, an alliance should be made between Britain and the Soviet Union to counter the Teutonic danger.

The Communist Party's adoption of the Popular Front provided the Labour leaders with an opportunity, tongue in cheek, to take up a left stance, upbraiding the communists for their reactionary line. Clem Attlee, tongue in cheek, exposed the central Communist Party fallacy:

> *The plain fact is that a Socialist Party cannot hope to make a success of administering capitalism because it does not believe in it. That is a fundamental objection to all the proposals that are put forward for a Popular Front in this country.*[2]

Herbert Morrison went even further and described the anomalous position that the Popular Front placed the communist leaders in. After telling delegates to the 1937 Labour Party conference he disagreed with Trotsky, Morrison nevertheless said he accepted Trotsky was a socialist. Amid laughter from delegates, he then asked:

> *Would Mr Pollitt appear on a platform with socialist, working-class Trotsky? He would not. If some of the leaders of the POUM in Spain, a working-class party, came to London, and the ILP wanted another United Front platform with them and Mr Pollitt, Mr Pollitt would not appear. But Mr Pollitt will appear with the Duchess of Atholl.*[3]

One of the Scottish land-owning aristocracy, the Duchess of Atholl was a staunch Conservative, one the Celtic nobility who sought to keep the lesser orders under control. Yet, in the popular press she acquired the sobriquet of 'the red Duchess'. This was because she greatly admired Joseph Stalin, believed he had made the Soviet Union highly democratic and thought Russia had become a powerful force for peace. She frequently spoke alongside communists on Popular Front platforms. When this brought her into conflict with her

---

1. Roger Hollis account of the CPGB appeared in MI5 Report No. l, 24th October 1940.
2. Clement Attlee, *The Labour Party in Perspective*, London, 1937, pp. 123-4.
3. Labour Party conference report 1937, p. 163.

own constituency party, she resigned as Member of Parliament for Kinross & West Perthshire. In the ensuing by-election, she stood unsuccessfully as an independent Conservative candidate, receiving support from Churchill and the Communist Party. Trotskyists used the opportunity furnished by the contest to expose her: Frank Maitland's pamphlet trenchantly argued she stood not simply for exploitation but for the continuation of semi-feudalism in the region. They sought to strengthen working-class organisation in that part of Scotland to combat it.[1]

Thanks to the Popular Front line, some members of high society, wanting to be daring and chic, not only flirted with the Communist Party but also with its fellow travelling organisations. Cyril Connolly satirised this in a piece entitled 'Where Engels Fears to Tread':

> *It was late last night when my lord came home*
> *enquiring of his lady-O*
> *The servants cried, on every side,*
> *She's gone to the Left Book Club Study Circle-O!*

The Left Book Club in that period was close to the Communist Party. Along with Victor Gollancz, two fellow travellers—Harold Laski and John Strachey—selected the books. The local groups were even more under Communist Party dominance. As Dr John Lewis, the convener of Left Book Club groups and himself a communist, explains in his history, *The Left Book Club*, all full-time organisers belonged to the Party. He goes on to say it proved to be a useful vehicle for establishing links with individuals with different class and political backgrounds. "The Left Book Club", he explains, "was only one section of the informed opinion which had urgently pressed for a military alliance with Russia". Then Dr Lewis cites Lord Cecil, Duncan Sandys, Wilson Harris of *The Spectator*, and Dingle Foot, who were prepared to be openly associated with it; other Tories and Liberals privately expressed their backing.[2] In either case, an entree had been gained into the political establishment, greater strength had been given to the *Daily Worker*'s demand for the overthrow of Chamberlain's government and its replacement by progressive politicians from all parties, more sympathetic to the Soviet Union.

So the Communist and the Labour Parties, whatever their differences, had one vital thing in common—a denial that their policies should be based on the bedrock principle of class struggle. They simply sought to shuffle the existing pack of cards, not to introduce new class forces through struggle. To revolutionaries, this was merely a symptom of their political bankruptcy: only by mobilising the working class, struggling to destroy capitalism, could peace be attained.

In 1938, the Fourth International began its transitional programme with the sentence: "The World political situation as a whole is chiefly characterised by

---

1. Frank Maitland's pamphlet, *Searchlight on the Duchess of Atnoll*, Revolutionary Socialist Party, Edinburgh, 1938.
2. John Lewis, *The Left Book Club: a Historical Record*, London, 1970, pp. 63, 114.

a historical crisis in the leadership of the proletariat".[1] Within a few months, this statement was tragically vindicated. The leaders of social democracy and Stalinism capitulated, doing nothing to stop an imperialist war from which the working class could gain nothing but lose their precious lives.

1. *Documents of the Fourth International: The Formative Years, 1933-40*, New York, 1978, p. 180.

THE VOICE OF FREE DEMOCRACY

Britain and the Blitz

On September 7th 1940, the Conway Hall in London was packed. John McGovern, MP, had just started to speak. He told his audience that the war was not a struggle between Democracy and Dictatorship. It was a capitalist-imperialist war, a fight of have-empires against have-not empires. At that moment, the air-raid sirens wailed. Then the anti-aircraft guns opened up. German bombs started dropping. For fifty-three days, virtually continuously, day and night, the Luftwaffe pounded London.

Ordinary people's lives were suddenly disrupted. The normal difficulties experienced by working class families became immeasurably greater. Food shops opened less – their queues grew longer. Getting to school could be both dangerous for children and stressful for the parents. Trying to go to work could be hazardous: it could involve long hours of standing in vain at a bus stop, exposed to bomb and bullet, waiting for a bus that may have been cancelled or re-routed because of enemy action. And, of course, after arriving at work, there was no guarantee of getting home again. Bomb craters, fires, streets cordoned off, no transport – these were a few of the possible obstacles to be surmounted.

Nor would home necessarily be a secure refuge. Many of the worst raids happened at night. Once the air-raid warning had sounded, families would scurry off to whatever shelter they could find. Public protection remained exceedingly inadequate. Despite many building workers being unemployed, few deep underground shelters had been built. Admittedly, there were a greater number of brick-built shelters, situated above ground in the highway, that afforded a little protection from flying debris for persons trapped by a surprise attack. Most people, however, either had to make do within a flimsy Anderson shelter, which they dug themselves in the back garden, or to crouch beneath their kitchen tables. Popular pressure – an illegal campaign largely led by the left – forced the authorities to keep the tube stations permanently open. Thousands bedded each night on the platforms. Others, less fortunate, spent their nights sleeping under railway arches or in sunken warehouses. One of the most notorious of these was at Tilbury, where up to 14,000 people regularly dossed down, despite being disturbed by hawkers selling their wares and prostitutes plying their trade. On the Isle of Dogs, an American journalist found 8,000 people with only eight vile-smelling improvised toilets.[1]

But Britain was a class divided society. Not everybody had to endure these hardships. The American journalist, already mentioned, went from the Isle of Dogs to the Dorchester Hotel. There he discovered the management had converted the cellars into expensive luxury shelters. Nine peers slept there each night. One of them was Lord Halifax, the foreign secretary. Throughout the night, he stayed well supplied by a waiter with his favourite brand of whisky.[2] Their wives and lady friends tended to frequent part of the subterranean complex that had been turned into a games room. Other wealthy people arranged for their own private shelters to be built. The most expensive belonged to Mrs E.M. Rawcroft, 81-year-old millionairess, the daughter of Sir Edward Wills of Imperial Tobacco. Built in the garden of her mansion at Torbay, Devon, it cost £24,000 and never needed to be used. Costing a small fraction of this, yet still a sign of gross extravagance, was the Soviet ambassador's refuge from aerial attack – a mere £1,600. It aroused the socialist wrath of the *New Leader*: undiplomatically the editor reminded readers of Maisky's counter revolutionary past in Tsarist Russia as a member of the Black Hundreds, of the fact that he only joined the Bolsheviks after the October Revolution had been victorious, and he suggested Maisky's London shelter symbolised his privileged position that differentiated the Stalinist bureaucracy from the working class, both in Britain and the Soviet Union.[3]

Still greater safety than any shelter, however deep, however well protected, could provide, would be secured by adopting a simple expedient: sail away on a magic carpet of money to the peace and tranquillity of the United States. In his diary, Chips Channon, the heir to the Guinness fortune, described the scene at Euston station when he, along with other affluent parents, bid farewell to their offspring, as they boarded the boat train and began the journey to the New World: "There was a queue of Rolls Royces and liveried servants and mountains of trunks. It seemed that everyone we knew was there". Clive Ponting, in his book on 1940[4], gives an impressive list of those leaving this emerald isle, set in a silver sea, for safer climes. All sections of high society were represented: Lord Mountbatten sent his wife and children, cabinet minister Duff Cooper his son, John Julius Norwich, city magnates like the four Rothschild families and Sir Charles Hambro dispatched their children. There were even individuals who gained political fame – or should it be notoriety? – in a time yet to come: Paul Channon, destined to be Mrs Thatcher's Minister of Transport, Jeremy Thorpe to lead the Liberal Party, and Shirley Williams to become a Labour cabinet minister. An estimated total of 17,000 children left this country. The

1. Andrew Sinclair, *War like a Wasp: The Lost Decade of the Forties*, London, 1989, p. 55.
2. *Sunday Express*, September 8th 1940. Also, Andrew Sinclair, *ibid*.
3. *New Leader*, November 7th 1940 and May 3rd 1941.
4. Clive Ponting, *1940: Myth and Reality*, Cardinal Books.

intelligence services confidentially confided to the government a million parents would have availed themselves of the opportunity to send their children abroad, given the opportunity – or rather, they should have said the money.[1]

The existence of two Britains could not be illustrated better than by the fact that canine lives were more valued than most children's. The *Scottish Daily Express* announced that the aristocrats of Scotland's dog kingdom had been evacuated to the United States and the colonies. Not wanting to run the risk of rare strains being wiped out in air raids, many famous prize-winners and most of the older pedigree stock left "for the duration of hostilities".[2]

Evacuees from working-class homes did not receive such cossetted treatment. Dispatched to country areas, they were often unwelcome visitors, interlopers over-straining already inadequate facilities. Not only did the influx aggravate existing education and housing problems, it brought in individuals not adjusted to their new habitat. Some of the new arrivals, of course, came from problem families. In his novel *Put Out More Flags*, Evelyn Waugh has a cunning character who traipses some disreputable, dirty and delinquent evacuees from house to rural house, threatening to billet them on the unfortunate occupants unless he was given an inducement to do otherwise. It was a way, to put it in legal parlance, of gaining money by menaces. Yet, even well-behaved evacuees could constitute a threat: coming from unhealthy city slums, they might spread disease.

The tensions engendered quickly aroused conflict. In September 1939, a Tory MP complained about the verminous evacuees from Glasgow arriving in his constituency. This immediately evoked a furious outburst from George Buchanan, the Labour MP for the Gorbals: "You are taking the fathers to fight, yet you make and make villainous, slanderous statements about their children". The ILP Member for Glasgow Camlachie, Campbell Stephens, then joined in, providing instances of the shabby treatment often meted out to evacuees. He cited the example of 150 mothers and children, dumped in a cold village hall and given straw or dirty mattresses to sleep on. Only two toilets were provided. Yet nearby was the Duke of Argyll's castle virtually empty.[3]

The authorities found themselves assailed from all sides. The rural recipients, clamourously complaining, demanded the evacuees removal. Equally the evacuees themselves were often unhappy, not adjusted to their new environment and without the money for the train fares to visit their parents. The parents grumbled both because they did not have the time or money to visit their offspring as well as about their treatment. When in the first months of the war the massive air raids that were expected failed to materialise, the majority of evacuees started trickling home. As a result, most children had returned to the danger zones when, by the autumn of 1940, the German air raids began in earnest.

In some official quarters, the onset of the blitz in the autumn of 1940 occasioned signs of panic. Hurriedly, fresh evacuation plans were devised. One

---

1. Clive Ponting, *1940: Myth and Reality*, London, 1990, pp. 140-1.
2. *Scottish Daily Express*, July 4th 1940.
3. *Forward*, September 22nd 1939.

'This is your quota'

of these was to move children from London to Brighton. This was rather as if
the British generals in the Crimean war had ordered the cavalry from their barracks and to gallop in the direction of Balaclava... for their own safety. Dr R.L.
Worrall, Brighton's Medical Officer of Health, on his own initiative produced
a leaflet denouncing this lunatic move. The leaflet stated that the evacuation
only increased the danger to children since Brighton was 'in the front line'. For
his troubles, Dr Worrall – who, incidentally, was a pioneer of British Trotskyism – was fined £100 under a defence regulation and dismissed from his post as
Medical Officer of Health. But then, for officialdom, two embarrassing things
happened. First, Churchill, on a well-publicised visit to Brighton, used the same
phrase as Worrall, boasting that he had come "to the front line". The other
was that tragically a German bomb exploded in a cinema during a children's
matinee, killing many of the evacuees. Dr Worrall was reinstated and his fine
reduced to £5.[1]

At another southern city – Portsmouth – morale seems to have plumbed the
depths. Ordinary people's depression grew as they became accustomed to seeing the affluent leaving the city each night, not wanting to experience the dan-
gers of the bombing. Their exit was made more conspicuous by the fact that
there was only one road connecting Portsmouth to the mainland. However,
attacks did not happen simply at night. Often solitary German aircraft, largely
for nuisance value, would fly over to disrupt the city's economic activity. In or-

---

1. The Pied Piper, *Rats*, Left Book Club (1942), p. 88. Also, interview with Dr R.L.
Worrall, of Seven Oaks, July 12th 1992. Pied Piper was the nom-de-plume of J.P.W.
Mallalieu

der to lessen the impact of these irritating intruders the authorities refused to open the air raid shelters unless the threat was considered to be a serious risk. But their judgement could be flawed. On one occasion, a solitary aircraft's appearance proved to be merely the prelude to a full-scale raid. In terror, people ran to the shelters. These remained closed. Crowds clamoured to break open the locks as the police, under orders to keep the shelters closed, baton charged the anxious multitude. A riot ensued. As a consequence, many were injured and two men killed Later a protest meeting was held. A resolution was passed condemning police violence and calling for all shelters, both public and private, to be kept open. Captain R.E.B. Beaumont, Tory Member for Portsmouth Central, led a protest delegation to the Home Office.[1]

Sudden loud explosions, the result of anti-aircraft fire, caused people to rush to Bethnal Green underground station and resulted in the worst civilian disaster of the blitz. A woman with a baby it seems, apparently slipped on the badly-lit winding staircase. Those following piled on top of her, within a minute creating a mass of dying humanity. All told 173 lives were lost – 27 men, 84 women and 62 children. An official inquiry was held, but the home secretary kept its findings secret. A bland and unilluminating explanation was provided to Parliament: "The effect cause of the disaster was that a number of people lost their self control at a particularly unfortunate time and place". But survivors dispute there had been any panic. They point to the narrow entrance to the stairwell, a hazard that local people had, months before, drawn to the attention of the Home Office. It may be the authorities, opposed to the occupancy of underground shelters anyway, felt no compulsion to make entry easier. Even so, it left the local populace with a smouldering hatred. In 1993, a commemorative plaque was unveiled at the station's entrance. The *Sunday Observer*, giving many facts about the tragedy, headlined the article 'Bitterness Lingers at Worst Civilian Disaster of the War'. Until then, the Home Office had kept the cause and extent of the disaster secret. One of the survivors, Mrs Faull, recalled how the government sought to stifle protest: "My father went to 10 Downing Street with a petition. He was marched off by soldiers with bayonets".[2]

The bombing also sought to draw attention to other grievances festering away in British society. Opposed to sexual discrimination, Campbell Stephen complained in Parliament about the big difference in compensation awarded to men and women. A man totally disabled by enemy action received 32 shillings and sixpence a week whereas a women worker only got 22 shillings and six pence. Even worse, he argued, was the treatment of totally disabled housewives and old persons, who received nothing whatsoever. In official eyes, they made no economic contribution to society and hence their loss of limbs merited no compensation.[3]

The plight of old people in air raids was liable to be dire. They had never been included in any evacuation plans. Yet, in air raids their reduced mobility made

---

1. *New Leader*, December 7th 1940
2. *Sunday Observer*, February 20th 1993.
3. House of Commons, October 23rd 1939.

it more difficult to reach the security of shelters. The blind, deaf and senile may easily be terrified, disorientated and unable to comprehend what was happening. Fortunately for many with these handicaps, they lived in working-class areas, where a strong community spirit and tradition of mutual help existed.

Working-class dwellings, situated close to factories and other military targets, were more likely to be bombed than middle-class estates, located in the leafy suburbs. Even so, sometimes the latter did receive the unwelcome attention from the Luftwaffe. Then the authorities tended to apply a discriminatory policy. Kingsley Martin, in the *New Statesman* observed the differential treatment:

> People dug out of their shelters (in the West End) are immediately taken off by taxis to hotels, given hot drinks and warm beds in an underground shelter – so they should be. Some of these people in East London wandered about for thirteen hours, having lost all their possessions in the world except what they stood up in, and were directed to a series of addresses which involved as much as eight miles walking before they were cared for.[1]

Newspapers carried headlines like 'Homeless East Enders Don't Know Where to Go' and 'Abandoned Us – Cry London's Homeless'. In the capital an estimated 80,000 people had been made homeless by the bombing. Some were forced to sleep at Epping Forest in the open air. Herbert Morrison, the home secretary, was exhorted to compile a register of empty dwellings. But he seemed more concerned to retain the men of property's goodwill, not the people's. Some landlords still expected tenants to pay rents – indeed some were even increased – when the houses were unfit for human habitation. In face of official inactivity, the Left called for direct action: 'Take Over the Shelters and Houses of the Rich' shouted the *New Leader* headlines.[2] Squatting, though rarely mentioned in the Press, became regarded by many as the answer to homelessness, even to just overcrowding. By 1942, an estimated 40% of Britain's housing stock had been destroyed or damaged. The bad prewar housing problem had become immeasurably worse.[3] The temptation to occupy unoccupied dwellings grew greater. Either because its slender resources did not stretch to it or because it did not wish to court the unpopularity that would inevitably accompany a policy of confrontation, the Home Office did not resort to evictions. Squatting was largely overlooked.

The government was worried about the growth of nests of sedition, bands of angry and disaffected individuals who challenged the basic tenets of capitalist society. In particular, the authorities feared what might happen in air raid shelters, where many huddled together, spending many hours when conversations might take place unsupervised as well as uncensored. Long boring nights in subterranean blackness might drift along dangerous revolutionary lines. The fears were not entirely groundless. People started taking matters into their own hands. In some places those taking refuge published their own magazines,

---

1. *New Statesman*, October 5th 1940.

2. *New Leader*, September 19th 1940.

3. *Plebs*, February 1945.

such as the *Hampstead Shelterers' Bulletin*. Partly through these publications but also through discussions with others elsewhere facing the same problems, a network of contacts throughout London grew up. In November 1940, a conference was held. A total of 79 delegates from 50 shelters decided to form the London Underground Station and Shelterers' Committee. They elected Harry Ratner, a Trotskyist, as chairman, and Alfie Bass, of the Communist Party, (later to become well known on television) as secretary.[1]

The Committee's immediate task was to protect existing shelters from official incursions. Smarting from the fact that people, by direct action, had illegally occupied underground stations, the authorities wanted gradually to claw them back. They attempted to carry out evictions under the pretext of 'clearing the passages and stairs'. They also sought to re-establish their authority and regain the initiative by settling any disputes between inmates that might arise. Aware that once this outside interference had secured a foothold there was no saying where it would end, the London Committee set up self-governing local shelter committees where they did not already exist. The inmates themselves democratically formulated the rules. Marshals were elected to enforce them. Order came out of chaos. The squalid scene, already mentioned, that was witnessed by the American journalist at Tilbury had been completely transformed. Tom Harrisson, the pioneer of Mass Observations, reported the community had become self-regulating. He found "laws enforced not by police and wardens (who at first proved helpless in the face of the multitudes), but generated by the shelterers themselves".[2]

As what had started out as a random assortment of individuals began to develop a feeling of collective identity and comradeship, they acquired a sense of their own power. People had to be listened to and their demands taken seriously. When they called for improvements to existing shelters, they struck a responsive chord throughout many parts of society. Even a correspondent of *The Times* echoed their views: Guy Clutton-Brock said the shelters were:

> *lacking dryness, warmth, satisfactory sanitation arrangements, adequate lighting and ventilation, washing facilities, bunks, canteens, health services, children's corners and, in fact, all those things which, it would appear, could easily have been provided during the last three months while the greatest evil is over crowding, which can only be relieved by the provision of additional small communal shelters for which there are plenty of sites available.*[3]

Bumbling incompetence appeared to lurk behind official attitudes. The failure to construct sufficient shelters seemed inexcusable: in July 1940 57,000 building workers remained unemployed. Government spokesmen then blamed shortages, bottlenecks that impeded progress. But the public's mood grew increasingly restive, unwilling to be fobbed off by governmental blarney. An angry audience at a Midlands' civil defence conference heard a novel method of

---

1. *New Leader*, 16, November 30th and December 28th 1940.
2. Tom Harrisson, *Living Through the Blitz*, 1978, pp. 118-9.
3. *The Times*, December 22nd 1940.

overcoming the shortage of cement. E.W. Barnes, the Bishop of Birmingham, bemoaned the fact that in this country the people did not possess the draconian powers Hitler did in Germany. Amid cheers, he told delegates that the Nazi authorities would not tolerate the cement shortage that existed here: they would simply shoot six manufacturers – those who remained alive would then quickly ensure abundant supplies of cement were always available in future.[1]

Poor quality bricks and shoddy construction also proved to be a problem. By a piece of skulduggery, the officials of Bradford City Council arranged meetings at times when the four ILP representatives could not attend. The four excluded councillors resolved to use the extra spare time by conducting their own survey of the city's street shelters. When they pronounced many of them sub-standard, the Lord Mayor dismissed it as just alarmist talk. So the ILP-ers enlisted the assistance of scientists from Bradford Technical College. Their investigation revealed twenty-eight shelters with soft bricks, four with loose bricks, forty-six with soft mortar and thirteen with structural weaknesses. Two things then happened that underlined their findings. First, one of the shelters simply collapsed when no Luftwaffe aircraft was within 100 miles of Bradford. Second, Professor J.B.S. Haldane, one of Britain's most eminent scientists, visited Yorkshire. He was pictured in the local Press crushing a brick taken from a Bradford shelter in the palm of his hand. Bradford's embarrassed Lord Mayor then wrote to the four ILP councillors congratulating them "for substantiating the suggestion that certain shelters in Bradford have been jerry-built".[2]

Much worse than shoddy shelters was to have none at all. Regarded as beyond the range of the Luftwaffe, Plymouth's civil defence remained an extremely flimsy, half-hearted affair. Its citizens were quite unprepared when the heavy German raids occurred. Widespread confusion and panic was still gripping the city – the authorities, too shocked, had taken no steps to evacuate the population – as the Luftwaffe delivered four more heavy blows. Completely overwhelmed and under-resourced, the authorities feebly attempted to evacuate women and children in private cars, many of which ran out of petrol thereby clogging the exit roads. Slightly before the final raid, Whitehall officials arrived to survey the scene. They found many survivors, cold and dazed, sleeping out rough on the moors. Assessing the tragedy in the *Daily Herald*, an angry Richie Calder wrote: "Somebody should be impeached for the cruel chaos which followed the Plymouth blitzes". He suggested Herbert Morrison and Ernest Brown were suitable candidates.[3]

Sleeping out, clad only in a nightie, or a few hastily snatched clothes, was a greater ordeal for the very young and the very old. This especially applied where deprivation and poverty had already undermined bodily well-being. In more northerly cities, accustomed to winter temperatures below freezing point, a further dimension was added to the suffering. In Glasgow, for example, Dr Nora Wattie, the child welfare officer, reported infantile mortality had

1. *New Leader*, December 7th 1940.

2. *Ibid*, April 4th 1941.

3. *Daily Herald*, May 3rd 1941.

been 93.1 per 1,000 live births in 1938; from January to June 1941 the figure had shot up to staggering 131.5.[1] Doubtless, air raids like the one lasting nine hours one night, with one of five hours the following night, helped to push up the numbers of those who died as an indirect consequence of the bombing as well as of the bombing itself. Terrified families in the Gorbals, huddled in the squares, surrounded by the large tenements, could hear their world crashing down around them. Even the all-clear did not end anxiety: there remained unexploded bombs among the rubble.

To bolster civilian morale, government propaganda boasted German cities were being bombed, too. In a recent raid of Hamburg, there had been what was termed 'a bombers' moon': the full moon completely illuminated the city, allowing the pilots to pick out their targets easily while it kept them hidden, in the inky blackness above, from the enemy anti-aircraft batteries. But, as the *Glasgow Forward* pointed out, exactly the same weather conditions prevailed when Glasgow received its severe poundings. The paper thought it was sure the working men and women of both Glasgow and Hamburg could agree at least on one thing – a resolution to abolish the moon.[2]

In fact, the British people generally were far from wholeheartedly endorsing a vindictive let-the-Germans-bastards-have-it attitude. The areas that tended to be bloodthirsty were those that had not themselves experienced bombing. An opinion poll that appeared in the *New Chronicle*, of May 17th 1941, reported that 45% of people in inner London wanted to see the reprisal bombing of Germany whereas 47% did not. By a small majority, the 'Noes' had it.

In the destruction of the blitz, three significant attitudes developed among working people:

First, there was the growing sense of community, the feeling of mutual dependence, a new realisation of one another's problems and aspirations were exceedingly similar. In air raid shelters people barriers broke down, strangers became friendly with persons they had never dreamt of even speaking to under normal circumstances. In an emergency, a person you did not know might risk his (or her) life to save yours. No wonder a sense of solidarity, of common purpose, emerged from this baptism of fire.

If a feeling of 'the great us' grew up among people of varying skills and status, there was, secondly, the contrary feeling of *them*, a hatred for those not making sacrifices – indeed, waxing rich – from the misfortunes of others. The black-marketeers, the fat cats, those who had positions and influence. The ruling class as well, who were responsible for the present mess and whose bumbling ineptitude had led to the war, seemed to be largely immune from any of war's ill effects. This widely held feeling may have been ill-defined. Nevertheless it was strongly held.

Third, through painful experience, people began to understand they had to do things themselves. No Labour leader would back any agitation. If you occupied an underground station, then it was no use appealing to Labour leaders.

---

1. *New Leader*, November 29th 1941.
2. *Forward*, March 18th 1941.

A prominent Labour right-winger, Herbert Morrison, as home secretary, remained responsible for the civil defence fiasco. He was assisted by the darling of the Labour left: Ellen Wilkinson was not merely Morrison's understudy, she also became his mistress. No Labour leader ever backed the illegal occupation of underground stations. No Labour leader ever backed illegal squats. Yet they occurred. People were resorting to do-it-yourself politics.

These were the rebellious seeds—nay, revolutionary seeds—that henceforth plagued British capitalism. The impact is revealed in later industrial and political unrest. It also created an attitude of critical hostility which pervaded society, resulting, among other things, in the defeat of Churchill-backed candidates in by-elections held in what had been rock solid Tory constituencies.

The Strange Execution of George Armstrong

A total of sixteen British subjects were executed as spies in the Second World War. The first to be hanged was George Johnson Armstrong. A 39-year-old merchant seaman, he originated from Newcastle upon Tyne and belonged to the British Communist Party.

On February 21st 1941, Armstrong arrived in Cardiff aboard the Californian oil tanker, SS La Brea. Immediately he set foot ashore, Detective Superintendent Lowden Roberts arrested him. Under police escort, he travelled to London, where he remained on remand for almost three months. Armstrong appeared at the Old Bailey before Mr Justice Lewis on May 8 1941. Tried in camera, he was found guilty and sentenced to death. His appeal was dismissed on June 23 1941. He climbed the scaffold at Wandsworth prison on July 10 1941.

All the above information appeared in Nigel West's book, *MI5*.[1] A writer who specialises in intelligence matters, Nigel West is the *nom de plume* of Rupert Allason, the Tory MP. Somehow, it seemed to me, this information did not ring true. Feeling suspicious, I tried to secure a report of the trial. Neither court records nor newspaper reports were available. This merely served to heighten further my suspicions.

Admittedly, after the Molotov-Ribbentrop pact, the British Communist Party did not support the war effort. But hitherto I had heard no allegation that its members spied for the Germans. In any case, on June 22nd 1941, the situation had been totally changed by Hitler's savage invasion of Russia.

Far from being an evil empire, the Soviet Union overnight was transformed, to use Winston Churchill's immortal words, into "our gallant Russian ally". A euphoric wave of pro-Soviet sentiment swept the country. The top West End stores flew the Red Flag. The Cossack marching song and 'My Lovely Russian Rose' emerged on radio as top of the pops.

---

1. Nigel West, *MI5*, London: Panther, 1983, pp. 321-3.

British communists responded to the sudden and unexpected surge in their public popularity by speaking on Conservative platforms at by-elections, strike-breaking in industrial disputes, and physically assaulting individuals who dared to criticise the Churchill government from a left-wing standpoint.

Aware of the mood prevailing at that time, I realised that, by July 10th 1941, George Armstrong – if he were a member of the Communist Party – must have been fervently patriotic and pro-war. Probably, before he was executed as a spy, the last words he shouted would be: "Long live our glorious war leaders, Winston Churchill and Joseph Stalin".

But was Armstrong a communist? My doubts were kindled by my failure to discover any confirmatory leads. Local Communist Party records on Tyneside do not contain his name. None of the old-timers could recall him. Likewise nationally: Communist Party officials seemed genuinely surprised when I drew their attention to Nigel West's book. None had ever heard of George Armstrong or the incidents described. The main charge used against him at his trial arose from an alleged conversation he had with a representative of the German consulate in Boston, Massachusetts. He was seen talking with a German official in a public park. Allegedly, he offered the stranger information about Atlantic convoys. Undercover British agents, working in liaison with the FBI, monitored this happening in a public park.

It remains unclear if it was a chance meeting so far as Armstrong was concerned, just meeting a total stranger when out for a walk, or what sensitive information was supposed to have been imparted. The authorities also stated that Armstrong jumped ship, assumed the name of George William Hope, and had been living in the United States illegally. The British authorities successfully sought his extradition.

But could Armstrong have committed the offence of divulging official secrets? I received a letter from Mr James S. Thompson, of South Shields, a mate of his who sailed with him on his last voyage. He claims that Armstrong did not have access to classified information. He was not in a position to give away information of value to the enemy. His trial and execution had merely been because the authorities wanted to set an example to other seamen. They had to remain tight-lipped, not giving vent to their opinions about the war.

Confirmation for this view came from the National Union of Seamen. Its former general secretary is Jim Slater, himself also a Tynesider and veteran of the wartime Atlantic convoys. In his younger days Jim Slater confesses that he possessed a strong Geordie accent. As a consequence, when he landed at Boston, American officials thought he was speaking an obscure form of Serbo-Croat and arrested him as a Yugoslav spy!

Jim Slater contends a strange mixture of paranoia and laxity over security then prevailed. In those days, America was not at war. The majority of its people did not want to see the USA become embroiled in a dispute that they regarded as an essentially European matter. Boston's bright lights shone. Its inhabitants continued to enjoy themselves, speaking freely, and not unduly worried whether any stray remarks might have some effect upon some far-distant conflict. But President Roosevelt and his administration thought the interests of America demanded it did not allow Britain to go down to defeat. Consequently, it gave aid to Britain, much of it covert, and the US intelligence services closely cooperated with its British counterparts.

While obviously Britain would rather the United States were an open ally in the war, nevertheless its status as a neutral did have some advantages. It meant that British convoys, leaving Boston, could hug the American coast for as long as possible, thereby prolonging their immunity from U-boat attack. This, in turn, meant that any American with a pair of good binoculars – and Nazi sympathies – could obtain, standing on the New England coast, an accurate idea of maritime movements. Such an individual would be much better placed than Armstrong to inform Berlin about British shipping.

A decisive reason, Jim Slater contended, for believing Armstrong to be innocent was that there was a set procedure for all convoys leaving the United States. Only when a vessel had left shore did the captain, in the presence of another officer, break the seal and open the envelope containing the sailing instructions. So the captain himself would not be in a position to betray convoy's secrets to the enemy, let alone an able seaman.

According to Nigel West, Armstrong had been greatly influenced by Molotov's speech to the seventh session of the Supreme Council. This urged workers involved in war work to down tools and dockers not to load troop ships. But Nigel West – and the prosecution at the trial – are making a travesty out of what Molotov said. Though he uttered a few platitudes about peace, he never asked workers to act in that way. The survival of the Soviet Union in those times depended upon bobbing and weaving among the capitalist nations. To have sought to arouse discontent among the underlings of other countries would have guaranteed universal condemnation, a hostility by other governments that would have threatened the very survival of the Stalinist ruling class.

It is true that George Armstrong, on arrival in Boston, Mass., did jump ship. He did become an illegal immigrant, assuming the false name of George William Hope. Under that guise, he did address meetings calling for direct action to be taken against war. But this was the line of Norman Thomas and the American Socialist Party, who desperately sought to keep America out of the war. Likewise a powerful left opposition emerged inside the National Maritime Union which regarded the war as an imperialist conflict. Among it were a lot of Trotskyists including, incidentally, a young seaman named Saul Bellow. It seems probable that Armstrong was influenced from this quarter rather than from Moscow.

T. Dan Smith, who sprang to national prominence as a guru of local government and went on to become, as its Public Relations Officer, the Labour Party's image-maker in the 1970s, knew the Armstrong family well. Until 1945, Dan Smith remained a prominent member of the Independent Labour Party. Throughout the war, the ILP argued that the struggle was over spheres of influence and markets, not over ideologies. As working men fell on the battlefield, the capitalists' profits rose at home.

According to Dan Smith, George Armstrong and his two sisters were influenced by the ILP's ideas. But they never became members, only sympathisers.

After their father's death, they took over the tripe business in the Newcastle's Grainger Market. At their stall, to ILP-ers like himself, they always gave preferential treatment. Occasionally, they might make donations to ILP funds. But none of them was ever active.

This may well have changed once George Armstrong joined the Merchant Navy. Experiencing the hardships and stress of Atlantic convoys, where ordinary seamen were forced to remain in the part of the vessel most vulnerable to enemy mines while passenger accommodation, next to the much safer officers' quarters, usually remained empty, might have helped him to find his voice. Likewise the treatment of coloured sailors, the blatant racism, must have been repellent to anybody with a shred of socialist principles.

Seamen aboard oil tankers had another grievance. In any naval engagement, they were sitting on top of their own crematorium One torpedo, shell or even tracer bullet could blow them to smithereens. Yet, they were expected to endure this immense danger for a pittance of pay, and at a time when the big oil companies' profits continued to rise and rise.

No wonder there was mass discontent. Besides individual seamen leaving their ships in American ports and failing to return, US newspapers and intelligence reports contain evidence that show anger among British seamen was rife. At Baltimore, for example, an unofficial meeting, attended by 500 men, protested about poor pay, poor food, poor conditions.

Into this inflammatory situation the *Daily Mirror* appeared to have accidentally stumbled. It printed a cartoon by Zec which depicted two seamen on a raft – their vessel, an oil tanker, had been torpedoed – and floating by was a piece of newspaper with the headline that petrol prices had risen two pence a gallon. So affronted by this cartoon were government ministers that the cabinet seriously considered using its wartime regulations to ban the *Daily Mirror*.

Up till now, when historians have discussed the possibility of taking the draconian move to ban the *Daily Mirror*, they have discussed the issue in terms of the affect Zec's cartoon might have had on civilian morale, but probably much more serious was its impact on the merchant marine, the fear that Britain's oil and other vital supplies could be disrupted. It could well have been this that made the authorities not only contemplate banning the *Daily Mirror* but also to taking action against a Tyneside seaman.

What the exact thing was that jogged George Armstrong to express political views that hitherto remained dormant may always remain a mystery. But what is clear is that he spoke as a socialist, not a Stalinist or Nazi. At his trial, the prosecution tried to portray him as an enemy agent. Translated into a contemporary analogy: it would be as if a British subject who campaigned against war in the Gulf were hanged as a spy of Saddam Hussein.

Even in the limited conflict that has happened in Northern Ireland, there have been numerous miscarriages of justice. The Birmingham Six and the Guildford Four are merely the most recent of a long line. Would not the tensions generated by World War Two be immeasurably greater, increasing the temptation to manufacture evidence? And would not, amid the many wartime restrictions on information, the challenges to flawed evidence have less scope than they do now? In these circumstances, the likelihood of errors of judicial judgement appear to be much enhanced.

Remarks such as those made by another author, John Bulloch, closely associated with the intelligence services, hardly allay misgivings about the dubious procedures the authorities adopted. In his book, also entitled *MI5*, he writes:

> George Johnson Armstrong, the first Briton to be hanged, never did any spying at all. He was a ship's engineer, and while in America at the beginning of 1941 was seen by British Intelligence men talking with a member of the German Embassy staff responsible for espionage.[1]

Apparently, Bulloch considers that no secret information was conveyed. However, given the opportunity, he thinks Armstrong might have done!

This provides a peculiar insight into British 'justice'. Whatever criticisms may have been levelled against 'hanging' Judge Jeffreys, at the bloody assizes he only condemned to death those who had been actually involved in the uprising of 1685. Others who were not involved in the Monmouth Rebellion but might have been, if the opportunity had arisen, were left completely unharmed.

Also, Judge Jeffreys, very generously, allowed the accused to hear the charges against them. They were permitted to speak in their own defence. At least formally, His Lordship adhered to the rules of natural justice. But to Sir William Stephenson, head of MI6 in the United States during the Second World War, such principles of natural justice were an anathema. When, a few months before George Armstrong's trial, he suspected another British seaman of passing information to the Germans, Stephenson transformed himself into judge, jury and executioner. He arranged for a hapless suspect to be murdered. Not only that – he boasted about it. "The FBI thought he was joking until the man was found dead in the basement of an apartment building".[2]

Anybody naive enough to think the shoot-to-kill policy is a new policy that began in Northern Ireland should turn to *A Man Called Intrepid*, the biography of Sir William Stephenson. At first glance, this may seem a peculiar title for a book about a man who was officially the head of British passport control in the United States. But that was merely his cover. In fact, he led a group of the British intelligence officers who behaved like Chicago gangsters. Indeed, to say this may well be a libel of Al Capone, who is not in a position to answer back.

Postscript:

Richard Crossman, the Labour leader and cabinet minister, used to write a regular weekly column in *The Times*. In an article published on May 16th 1973, he wrote that, during the Second World War, only two spectacular innovations were made in the techniques of warfare. The first was the ability to destroy

---

1. William Stevenson, *A Man Called Intrepid: The Secret War*, Macmillan, 1976, p. 120.
2. John Bulloch, *MI5: The Origin and History of Britain's Counter Espionage Service*, London, Arthur Barker, 1963, p. 173.

an entire city in a night by aerial bombardment. The other, he wrote, was the only one in which:

> ... *the British achieved real pre-eminence. We trained a small army of gifted amateurs for all the dirtiest tricks from lying, bugging, forging and embezzlement to sheer murder – all, of course, in the name of preserving the democratic way of life.*[1]

Though too modest to tell the readers of *The Times* about his own role, it is true that Crossman figured prominently in these sleazy undercover, underworld operations. Ellic Howe's book, *The Black Game*, devotes an entire chapter to Crossman.[2] Almost certainly, he never belonged to His Majesty's Death Squads, but probably this moderate Labour politician was an accessory before and after the fact to some of the murders they committed.

---

1. My emphasis - RC
2. Ellic Howe, *The Black Game: British Subversive Operations Against the Germans During the Second World War*, London: Queen Anne Press, 1982, Ch. 5, 'Enter Mr Crossman'.

Reprinted from "SOCIALIST APPEAL," April, 1942.

REMEMBER HONG KONG
And all this too . . . .

The tales of the atrocities committed by the Japanese army upon British soldiers at Hong Kong have aroused the British masses as no atrocity story has done since the outbreak of the war.

And no wonder!   It is our husbands, sons, brothers and friends upon whom these terrible atrocities are being committed.

Even if we discount the exaggerations and falsifications of the British ruling class, the history of Japanese imperialist aggression against the Chinese people and the subsequent atrocities committed by the Japanese ruling class leave us with no doubt that they have indeed committed acts of barbarism on the bodies of captured British soldiers.

We publish here a photograph of the heads of a group of Chinese soldiers, severed from their bodies by the Japanese imperialists during the conquest of Manchuria. It was the left wing of the working class movement which published these pictures and tried to rouse the masses of the world to protest against this horrible aggression and accompanying outrages. But what were the journals of British imperialism saying? They were not interested in rousing the masses then! They were apologists for Japanese im-

A JAPANESE POSTCARD

A group of Chinese soldiers, their heads severed from their bodies by the Japanese in the Manchurian war. Why did the British Capitalists not protest then?

BRITISH ATROCITY IN BURMA

16 Burmese patriots beheaded by the British in Tharrawady in 1931, and publicly exhibited to terrorise the rest of the population. Is it surprising that in this district the Japanese are succeeding in gaining a large measure of aid from the population?

perialism and were justifying their actions! Each successive Government of British capitalism covered up the atrocities of their Japanese class brothers and official British spokesmen tried to minimise what was taking place, or even directly claimed that the Japanese were carrying civilisation into China.

Only a few months ago Mr. Churchill in the House of Commons admitted that the British Government had closed the Burma Road at the instigation of the Japanese Government. In this way they materially assisted the Japanese in extending their conquest of China, and are therefore responsible for the consequent atrocities. If they raise the question now it is not because they opposed the atrocity measures as such, as they would have us believe, but only because they hope to arouse the natural anger among the workers and use this hatred for their own reactionary ends.

Every imperialist government indulges in vile atrocities against the

Deep Waters in the Pacific

On December 7th 1941, Japanese pilots jubilantly shouted 'Tora! Tora!' as they dive-bombed the American naval base of Pearl Harbour. The result was devastating. Naturally, President Roosevelt reacted angrily. He told the US congress the surprise attack would live in the annals of history as an act of infamy.

In fact, this traditional version of events, to use Sir William Armstrong's delicious expression, is 'economical with the truth'. The United States had already intercepted Japanese messages. It therefore knew an attack was pending. Prudently, the US navy had sent its most modern vessels to sea. The Japanese bombed a junkyard. Deception and diplomacy go together under capitalism. The US government wanted to enter the Second World War. The trouble was that the majority of the American people saw the struggle as of no concern of theirs: they were peace loving and neutralist. Only a catastrophic atrocity would inflame passions, replacing the pacifist with warlike attitudes.

Why did Roosevelt and his advisers want to enter the conflict? It must be remembered that in the autumn of 1941 the outcome of the war was far from certain. To most Western advisers, it seemed probable the Soviet Union would topple under the Wehrmacht's onslaught. Russia's collapse would leave Hitler free to march into the Middle East, where he would control most of the Anglo-American oil supplies.

Such a calamitous loss would probably smash Britain's already fragile morale. With the surrender of Britain and the British navy falling under Hitler's command, Roosevelt envisaged a nightmare scenario, where Germany had control of virtually the entire Euro-Asian landmass. In such circumstances, the world would be ruled from Berlin, not Washington.

War remained the only means of dispelling this colossal danger. But it also provided the United States with the opportunity of dealing with two problems simultaneously. For if Germany was a threat internationally, Japan was a threat in the Pacific. The expanding interests of Nipponese and Yankee imperialisms increasingly conflicted.

Therefore, the White House decided to bring the issue to a head, forcing Japan into a corner by exposing its fatal weakness – its great dependency upon imported raw materials. Once an oil embargo was imposed on July 31st 1941, the time bomb had begun ticking: Japan's rulers had no alternative but to fight. The longer they delayed, the weaker Japan's economy would become while her adversary garnered fresh strength.

The British government's policy arose from its desperately weak position. Above all else, it wanted to entice the United States to enter the war. Only then would it stand the remotest chance of winning. In the meantime, however, while America remained a non-combatant, inevitably Britain's preoccupation was with the struggle in Europe. It had not the resources to withstand Japanese pressure in the Far East. Consequently, Churchill & Co. resorted to appeasement, hopeful this would dissuade Emperor Hirohito from gobbling up British colonial possessions.

Sometimes, the machinations of the British government ran into difficulties. For example, early in 1941 engineers in a Huddersfield factory thought all their hard labour and overtime was going to help the war effort. And they were right – it was! But they only discovered which war effort when one day, quite by accident, a cover fell off a piece of equipment and a worker read the notice that was underneath: "For the inspection of the Japanese army". Production immediately came to a halt. The Huddersfield Amalgamated Engineering Union district committee, then a militant organisation led by the Warwick brothers, backed the shop stewards and raised the issue nationally. The dispute was only resolved when Churchill gave a personal assurance the trade would henceforth be terminated.

But this did not happen in every instance. A lot of equipment and material from this country got through. To give one example: any British sailor torpedoed by a Japanese submarine had the consolation, as he went under for the third time, of knowing that the periscope contained the finest British workmanship – Barr & Stroud, of Glasgow, takes pride in producing only the best.

Even with the beginning of hostilities, Anglo-Japanese cooperation continued. In cities like Hong Kong and Shanghai, big commercial centres where key posts were held by Westerners, it was in their mutual interest to retain the existing structures. The Japanese government, wanting to exploit the parts of China its army had occupied and not having the time to train and replace top or middle management who happened to be white, adopted a conciliatory approach. From the standpoint of British capitalism, it also made sense for them to keep the key jobs in these ports. Not only could money be made during the war – and profits quietly sent home once it was all over – but, when peace returned, British companies would be well placed to assert their predominant influence again.

On June 22nd 1942, the manager of the Shanghai branch of a British export house somehow succeeded in getting a letter through to his relatives in this country: "We are doing good business with our Japanese customers... We are being exceedingly well treated here – no restrictions whatever and we have no complaints". The backers of British blood sports must have been cheered when their journal, *Horse and Hounds*, informed them that in Hong Kong the Japanese occupation authorities had permitted horse racing, an immensely popular sport in the colony, to continue, though they did stipulate 30% of the tote's takings should go to the Japanese army.

Striving to foster goodwill, officers of the occupying army fraternised and endeavoured to play Western games. In the case of billiards, this had somewhat bizarre consequences. As the Japanese tend to be of small stature, they had difficulty striking the ball and so ordered that part of all the billiard table's legs should be sawn off. The *Glasgow Forward* reported the amputations under the ironic heading: 'Another Japanese Atrocity'.

Of course, all this is a world away from the experiences of the hapless prisoners toiling away – and dying – on the Burmese railway. Or, for that matter, soldiers involved in battle. The war was characterised by a savage barbarism, an unprecedented racism that acted as a justification for any atrocity.

The British media highlighted the war crimes of the enemy. The white-skinned Europeans were clearly superior to the sub-human orientals. No criticism was made when Admiral Halsey issued the command to his men: "Remember Pearl Harbour – keep them dying". Or when he ordered aircraft to machine-gun survivors from torpedoed Japanese ships in the water. These slit-eyed yellow men were sub-human. They deserved all they got.

But there was another voice in Britain, one of those opposed to the war. Journals like the Trotskyist *Socialist Appeal* argued that British imperialism was every bit as bad, if not worse, than its Japanese counterpart. Courageously, it printed a leaflet showing that British troops had used the same methods as the Japanese. A photograph of Burmese peasants, beheaded because of their opposition to the British Raj, was included to rub home the point. It led to an outburst of rage in the Press. Members of Parliament called for the *Socialist Appeal* to be banned. But threats failed to silence it.

Equally, the *New Leader*, organ of the ILP, proclaimed its internationalist stand. The ILP's Japanese counterpart had been smashed, its leaders executed in 1937, because it opposed Japanese aggression against China. Nevertheless, this did not prevent the *New Leader* editorial, immediately after Pearl Harbour, sending its greetings to, and expressing its solidarity with, Japanese socialists, scattered though they be, who were also fighting for same principles.

One article, paraphrasing Trotsky's famous order to the Red Army in 1919 always to remember that there were two Englands, declared there were two Japans: the Japan of the reactionary emperor, about whose person superstitions had been woven into a reactionary religion, the industrial magnates who dominated the economy, and the warlords, who sought to force every citizen into their militaristic mould. But there was also another Japan, of workers who formed clandestine organisations to fight for better living standards, of socialists who strived to overthrow the existing system of exploitation, and of those opposing the imperialist war. This second Japan was our Japan, the power that ultimately contributed to the creation of socialism throughout the world.

Of course, it was precisely this second Japan that Allied governments after 1945 wanted to prevent from triumphing. So, once Japan's rulers had acknowledged their defeat, their subordination to American imperialism, they were again re established in power. Emperor Hirohito and the giant Japanese industrial concerns were recalled to keep the lid firmly on a discontented society. In other words, those who ordered the attack on Pearl Harbour in 1941 were required after 1945, under Allied instructions, to attack the enemy at home – in other words, the Japanese working class.

Arms and the Man

Shortly after the Second World War began, a proposal was made whose implementation would have certainly led to instant revolution. This suggestion came from an unlikely source – the Economic League. Shortly afterwards, in January 1940, the War Office's journal, *Army Quarterly*, gave its support. What they proposed was that all British workers should receive swingeing pay cuts, reducing their wages to the same level as those 'enjoyed' by members of the armed forces.

Behind this move lay a sound but crooked logic. There was the realisation that military personnel constituted part of society, not immune from the pressures which influenced others. Compared to workers, soldiers almost certainly regarded their pay and conditions as poor. On top of this went the added hazards of violent death or being maimed for life.

Painful daily experience reminded the average conscript of his personal situation. Officers received much more money, better food, many privileges he was denied. He would find desirable places out of bounds to 'other ranks'. He would be left to stand in a crowded corridor of a railway compartments while officers sat in splendid first-class isolation.

From the government's standpoint, the hazards were heightened because the average soldier, besides continually rubbing up against injustice and privilege, had plenty of opportunity to discuss his grievances with his comrades. The armed forces does not merely reflect the tensions arising from the class divisions of society, at times of crisis it develops them in hothouse fashion. History is strewn with examples of insubordination and mutiny, of soldiers voting with their feet – and electing governments out of the barrels of their rifles.

Mindful of the potential danger, the authorities in the Second World War did their utmost to counteract subversion. The police and Special Branch kept remarkably close surveillance. Sometimes it even extended to analysis of the political content of graffiti on the walls of public lavatories.

An inspection of the minutes of England's Northern Region reveal some alarming reports reached the authorities. Members of HM Forces were openly reading Trotskyist literature. The slogan 'Put Lord Derby in the Front-Line' had been daubed outside Catterick barracks. At an ILP public meeting in Newcastle, plain clothes policemen stated that Frank Maitland told soldiers in the audience that:

> they were bloody suckers fighting for three shillings a day. I know because I was one for two years. You are the bloody suckers who are being exploited by the capitalist class.[1]

Poor pay did not only affect the soldier, all his dependents suffered as well. The wife of a serviceman received a paltry fourteen shillings a week, seven shillings of which was deducted from her husband's pay. Contrary to the findings of Rowntree and all other social investigators, who showed that poverty grew with the size of family, the War Office thought that, the larger the family, the less money would be needed per head. A mother received five shillings a week for the first child, three for the second, two for the third, and only a shilling for the fourth and all subsequent children. In 1943, the National Nutrition Council disclosed, in practical terms, what this meant. Its research in Edinburgh showed many soldiers' wives were too poor to buy their scanty food rations. They had not the money for two ounces of butter, four ounces of margarine, four ounces of bacon, an egg and the few other things they were entitled to per head on a weekly basis.[2]

Another source of discontent arose because, in one respect, the authorities were less generous than they had been in the First World War. Quite often, where there were low incomes, it was customary for grown-up sons to remain unmarried just so they could continue contributing to their parents' home. From 1914-18, the War Office recognised this fact, providing mothers with five shillings a week for unmarried sons serving in the armed forces. In the Second World War, the allowance was withdrawn.[3]

Feelings of bitterness grew when soldiers could compare their lot not only with industrial workers in this country, but also with fellow soldiers fighting on the same side. Australian and New Zealand troops received much higher pay. The contrast became most marked, however, when Britain experienced an influx of American GIs. An ILP leaflet entitled 'Salute the Soldiers With More Pay' said that whereas the British single man in the armed forces earned twenty-one shillings a week, his US counterpart got 70 shillings.

The criticism, though, did not merely come from the left. In 1942, a clutch of Tory MPs, most of them army officers, lambasted the government's defence of its low pay policy, saying it was "a disgraceful piece of jiggery pokery". Major John Profumo, who in the Sixties gave his name to a sex scandal, referred to

---

1. Northern Region, *Special Branch Security Work, No. 67*, July 31st, 1943.

2. *New Leader*, April 15th 1943.

3. *Plebs*, November 1939; *Daily Herald*, September 26th 1939.

the White Paper as a cowardly Yellow Paper. It helped, he said, to undermine morale throughout the services.[1]

But other grievances as well gnawed away at morale. Even those soldiers who accepted the considerable disparities in power and wealth discovered it difficult to sustain their beliefs when confronted with the ludicrous conduct of Britain's own commanders. In the First World War General Ludendorff said, "The British soldiers are like lions", and his aide-de-camp added, "Lions led by donkeys".[2] In the Second World War, the public perceived Colonel Blimp, a character created by the cartoonist David Low, as the embodiment of the typical army officer. Upper-class, ineffective and feeble, Colonel Blimp remained a prehistoric relic, handicapped by having gun-metal where normal human beings have brains. When in 1942 Winston Churchill discovered a film was being made about the life and times of Colonel Blimp, he expressed his intense annoyance: "I am not prepared to allow propaganda detrimental to the morale of the army, and I am sure the cabinet will take all necessary action". He even said he thought that cartoonist Low was a Trotskyist! But Churchill soon found out the film's production was common knowledge. To ban it would be counterproductive, merely heightening people's awareness of the deficiencies of the officer caste.[3]

By then, British generals had already strewn the battlefields with disaster after disaster. In the spring of 1940, the British sent an expeditionary force to Norway. Its objective was to interdict supplies of Swedish iron ore, vital to the German war effort, which in the winter months had to be shipped through the Norwegian port of Narvik since the Baltic was frozen over. Initially, news of this move aroused great enthusiasm in this country. Neville Chamberlain, then the prime minister, told a jubilant Parliament what a cruel blow had been struck against the enemy: "Hitler has missed the bus".[4]

Alas, Chamberlain's optimism was not shared by soldiers on the expedition. They had been landed in the Arctic circle with no snow-shoes or skis. They did not even have maps of the region. Some of them were disembarked at the wrong place. On arriving on Norwegian soil, a lot of soldiers faced the prospect of fighting the enemy with their bare hands: nobody had bothered to see that guns left Britain along with the troops. To cap all the chaos, the two commanders—Admiral the Earl of Cork-and-Orrery and General Mackay—had quarrelled and were no longer speaking to each other. A full catalogue of the cock-ups is given in François Kersaudy's recently published book, *Norway 1940*: it shows it was hardly surprising that the German army won.[5]

Of course, much worse was to follow later the same year. The German Wehrmacht, using its panzer divisions and new blitzkrieg techniques, swiftly brushed

1. *Labour Monthly*, June 1942.
2. Alan Clark, *The Donkeys*, p. 157.
3. Paul Addison, *The Road to 1945*, p. 132; David Irving, *Churchill's War: The Struggle for Power*, Western Australia. 1987, p. 301; Keith Middlemass, *Politics in Industrial Society*, 1978, p. 358.
4. Neville Chamberlain, Speech, House of Commons, April 9th, 1940.
5. Francis Kersaudy, *Norway* 1940, *passim*.

the Allies aside. France fell; to avoid extinction the British Expeditionary Force fled for its life: an armada of a thousand little boats evacuated 300,000 men from Dunkirk. To explain this humiliating defeat, for a long time the British Establishment has peddled conveniently a myth. It all happened, they argue, because Britain was ill prepared for war in 1939. In fact, it was defenceless. Not only did this remove the blame from government ministers and military top brass, placing responsibility on the shoulders of their left critics of the 1930s, but also has anti-left implications for politics in post-war Britain. This country, they continue, must not be caught unprepared again. Throughout the Cold War, therefore, Britain has maintained military expenditure at a higher proportion of GNP than any advanced industrialised country. It was one of the factors that retarded Britain's economic development compared to, say, that of Germany and Japan.

The entire edifice of this argument, however, is based on a lie. It was untrue to say that Britain in 1940 was unprepared, confronting the enemy onslaught with inadequate resources. Military historians, analysing the position when Hitler began his attack in 1940, give another, rather embarrassing, explanation. In their standard work on the Second World War, for example, Peter Calvocoressi and Guy Wint write:

> Hitler did not begin his attack in the west with any marked material superiority. The battle of France was won by superior skill and not crushing weight of numbers. In the vital department of tanks the Germans were numerically weaker with some 2,700, compared to almost nearly 3,000 French and 200 British. The quality of the tanks on the two sides was about the same. But in tactics and leadership the French and British were outclassed.[1]

After early Nazi advances, the Allies moved their headquarters, the nerve centre of all their military operations, back to the small village of Briare. A single telephone was the village's sole contact with the outside world. Its proud owner was the village postmistress. She shut up shop and went for a meal from midday to 2pm. Unfortunately, General Guderian and his panzer divisions, unaware that the rules of cricket establish the custom of a lunch break, just continued to advance. Later General Guderian admitted: "Contrary to the expectations of the German High Command, the attack in the West led to rapid and total victory".[2]

Incredibly, the lessons from the fall of France were not learned. It is as if His Majesty's Forces were under the command of General Oliver Hardy and Field Marshal Stanley Laurel. Ineptitude and overweening self-confidence resulted the following year in what Churchill termed "the worst disaster and largest capitulation in British history". Pervasive racism contributed to the catastrophe by helping further to befuddle the generals' already exceedingly dubious judgements. In 1941, Japan had entered the war. The British High Command believed in the inherent superiority of its own white skinned soldiers over their

---

1. Peter Calcocoressi and Guy Wint, *Total War*, 1972 ed., p. 116.
2. General Guderian, quoted in Werner Maser, *Hitler*, 1973, p. 291.

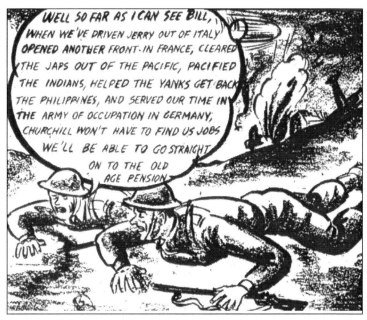

small, slit-eyed yellow-skinned opponents. A BBC news report carried a conversation between a group of officers. One of them remarked: "These Japs are bloody fools". This was then unanimously agreed. A second officer pointed to another of their disabilities: "Those Japs can't fly. They can't see at night and they are not well trained". A third conceded that the Japanese navy might have some good ships, but added: "They can't shoot".[1]

In these circumstances, the poor quality of their opponents presented the British commanders with peculiar problems. The Chief of Staff issued an order saying that "the Japanese should not be over-estimated". General Robert Brooke-Popham, head of all British forces in the Far East, lamented the lot of the British troops and asked: "Don't you think they are worthy of some better enemy than the Japanese?" Another general, eager for battle, expressed his worries to Brooke-Popham: "I do hope, sir, we are not getting too strong in Malaya because, if so, the Japanese may not attempt a landing".[2]

These fears soon proved to be groundless. Small groups of inscrutable Orientals, equipped only with bicycles, landed on various parts of the Malayan peninsular. Peddling away furiously and living off the rice they found in the fields around them, they defeated numerically much stronger detachments of the British army. Nemesis finally arrived with the fall of Singapore, where al-

1. John Costello, *The Pacific War 1941-1945*, 1981, pp. 106-10; Stanley W. Kirby, (1986) *The War Against Japan*, 1957, pp. 193-9.
2. John Dower, *War Without Mercy*, 1986, p. 99.

most all the guns had been facing in the wrong direction. The Japanese casualties were 3,507 dead and 6,150 wounded. They had defeated a British army of 138,708 soldiers, most of whom were taken prisoner.[1]

Singapore had been the pivot of British imperial power in the Far East. Its dramatic fall, and the humiliation of the white man's defeat, had a significance not lost on colonial people. It provided a great fillip to the anti-imperialist cause. Henceforward, the myth of white racial superiority, of imperialist invincibility, could no longer be plausibly sustained.

The fall of Singapore also sent earth tremors through the political scene in Britain. The government became highly unpopular. Most people blamed it for the mess the country was in. A public opinion poll taken in March 1942 found only 35% of people were satisfied with the government while 50% were dissatisfied. A teenage Margaret Thatcher must have been shocked when the safe Conservative seat of Grantham was lost in a by-election. During the early months of 1942, an unprecedented four Tory constituencies went the same way.[2]

Temporarily the ruling class was divided in itself, unsure whether to continue or to sue for peace. A highly volatile mixture of defeatism, demoralisation and rebellion affected personnel within the state machinery, particularly the army. There were ominous grumbles in the ranks of the working class as well.

Assessing the situation at the time, George Orwell wrote: "It seems to me that we are back to the 'revolutionary situation' which existed but was not utilised after Dunkirk". Eight months later, he had to report:

> Well, the crisis is over and the forces of reaction have won hands down. Churchill is firm in the saddle again. Cripps has flung away his chances, no other left-wing leader or movement has appeared, and what is more important, it is hard to see how any revolutionary situation can recur till the western end of the war is finished. We have had two opportunities, Dunkirk and Singapore, and we took neither.[3]

Orwell's comments need some clarification. The conditions for a revolution of the October 1917-type did not then exist in Britain. No workers' organisation, such as Soviets, had emerged, capable of wrestling power from the ruling class. However, uncertainty at the top combined with profound anger from below could easily have led to a February 1917 revolution or, to translate it into Orwell's terms, a Spain 1936 revolution. As his book *Homage to Catalonia* shows, experiencing the joyous freedom of the exploited people of Barcelona after the overthrowal of the hated old regime there was the great high spot of his life. Darkening shadows gradually extended over Orwell's personality as he slowly realised he would never see the same again.

---

1. S. W. Kirby, *Singapore: The Chain of Disaster*, 1971, pp. 73-5.
2. Paul Addison, 'By-elections in the Second World War', in C. Cook and Ramsden, *By-Elections in British Politics*, 1973, p. 201.
3. George Orwell, *Collected Essays, Journalism and Letters, 1940-1943*, ii, pp. 246, 317.

But in 1940, 1942, and again in 1945, it was a close run thing. The authorities were extremely nervous. The counter-measures they took along with a mixture of good luck and help from the labour and trade union leaders – always prepared to attempt to push protest along channels harmless to the system – helped to pull them through. How near British capitalism came to the abyss has always been officially played down. Documents have been suppressed. Half-truths told. As I get down to writing the hidden history of the Second World War, increasingly I realise that all the embarrassing 'black holes' were not only dug by Stalin. Churchill and his henchmen were excellent diggers, too.

'Go – My Boy. Defend your freedom! And MY CASH!'

The Enemy Within

Early in November 1944, when I was in my mid-teens, I attended a public meeting of the Lancaster branch of the Independent Labour Party. Guy Aldred journeyed down from Glasgow to be the guest speaker. Not himself a member of the ILP, Aldred espoused a highly individualistic brand of libertarian socialism that made such conformity quite impossible. Both his appearance and manner seemed somewhat cranky to me. He wore Bernard Shaw-style plus-fours and possessed a raucous Scottish voice, with which he was able to put forward the most reasonable case in the most unreasonable manner.

Aldred had just branded Winston Churchill a mass murderer. He described how the war leader – or should it be war criminal? – gloated over women and children being burnt alive, a direct consequence of his order to the RAF to terror bomb the working-class districts of Hamburg. Then, suddenly, Aldred's oration was interrupted. The head of the local Home Guard strode on to the platform. Much taller and thinner than Captain Mainwaring of the television series *Dad's Army*, he nevertheless exuded the same authoritarian pomposity. For him, the gathering was an orgy of sedition that had to be terminated forthwith.

But the worthy officer of the Home Guard was in for an unpleasant surprise. Whereas normally his orders must usually have been obeyed without question, on this occasion they met merely with derision. Instead of meekly obeying, Guy Aldred unleashed a diatribe of invective and abuse not only against Churchill but also against his lackey from the Home Guard. The commanding officer certainly had never before been subjected to such a ferocious verbal tirade. Amid catcalls and boos, Captain Mainwaring retreated in confusion from the platform.

Immediately, the proceedings resumed without further interruption. However, unbeknown to the 70 or so in the audience, some of the local Home Guard were drinking in a nearby pub. They resolved to go down to sort out the ILP meeting. They knew how to deal with a bunch of cowards and traitors, using whatever force happened to be necessary to teach them a lesson.

I was sitting about the fourth row from the front when the Home Guard charged through the swing doors at the back of The Friends' Hall. A fight ensued. It was nasty, bloody, brutish and short. Within two minutes, the gallant men in khaki were fleeing in disarray.

Naturally, this defeat was very bad for Home Guard morale. In the following weeks these part-time soldiers kept their heads down, slinking around Lancaster, hoping to avoid the ridicule of the populace. They were afraid of being asked the embarrassing question: "If a few conchies can beat you up, what would happen if the Germans came?"

Actually, in the fight the Home Guard had acquitted itself quite well. A lot of conscripts were billeted in Lancaster and the surrounding district. Though it violated Army Regulations, leaving them open to severe disciplinary charges, many soldiers had acquired the habit of going to ILP meetings in their civilian clothes. Obviously the numbers and proportion of HM Forces attending ILP meetings fluctuated from week to week. It is impossible to say how many were at the Guy Aldred meeting. Usually about a quarter of the audience were soldiers.

When members of the Home Guard charged through the swing doors, with a Balaclava-like innocence, they unexpectedly found themselves in a very unequal battle. Physically fit young men, trained in unarmed combat, were pitted against older men, many of whom were out of condition. The younger men also had something to fight for – if their presence at the meeting became known to their officers, they might find themselves consigned to the glasshouse. So the outcome was hardly surprising.

But the Home Guard's humiliation must have started official minds ticking. Wasn't it rather strange, they must have thought, that so many people at the Guy Aldred meeting could fight so well? Eventually, they must have discovered the reason.

It had an important result. On the morning of December 19th 1944, four soldiers stationed in Lancaster Castle were told not to go on their normal duties. They were then arraigned before their commanding officer. Two plain-clothes policemen from Scotland Yard entered the room. They had journeyed up from London to question them about their political activities. The belongings of every soldier stationed at Lancaster had been searched without them knowing. ILP, Trotskyist and anarchist literature had been found in some lockers. Almost certainly, what disturbed the authorities the most was the discovery of evidence that moves were afoot to form soldiers' councils.

The *New Leader* of December 30th 1944, which gave the news of these developments, stated that other searches of soldiers' belongings had taken place at army barracks in the Midlands and East Anglia. The report went on to hint that *War Commentary*, the anarchist journal, seemed to be the main target.

The authorities had unearthed a network of contacts in the armed forces. With every copy of *War Commentary* sent to a serving soldier, a monthly newsletter was enclosed. John Oldny, a talented refugee from Nazi Germany, produced it. He had established a network of 200 contacts, mainly during his two years in the Pioneer Corp. Attractively produced and illustrated, the monthly newsletter strived to articulate many grievances of the armed forces and promote action against them. Soldiers' councils needed to be created.

Alongside this there was a plethora of pamphlets, including one entitled 'The Wilhelmshaven Revolt'. It gave an exciting account of the mutiny of the German navy that sparked off the German Revolution of 1918-19. Written under the nom-de-plume 'Icarus', the author, Ernst Schneider, had been a member of the Hamburg Workers' and Soldiers' Council. Describing those stirring events, his message was quite simple: go and do thou likewise.

Besides the anarchists, both the ILP and Trotskyist RCP maintained organised factions within the armed forces. The ILP Forces group, whose first secretary was Ken Eaton, followed by Cyril Hughes of Manchester, produced a regular bulletin. Besides having articles that dealt with grievances, such as bad food and poor pay, a writer with the nom de plume 'Bellerophon', discussed topics like street fighting and revolutionary military tactics. He pointed out that struggles would take place on the troops' home territory, where they would know the places of key military value. He stressed the importance of always striving to get soldiers and workers united in struggle. Even those who remained loyal to the capitalist system would be overwhelmingly workers. Propaganda along class lines, like Tom Mann's 'Don't Shoot' leaflet, should be directed at them.[1]

Obviously, the military authorities must not have remained oblivious about what was taking place. Discontent found extensive expression. Acts of insub-

---

1. *ILP Forces' Bulletin*, May and June 1945.

ordination were widespread. In various shapes and forms, incidents like that at Lancaster must have been repeated up and down the country. The powers-that-be felt compelled to make a pre-emptive strike, prosecuting the Trotsky-ists over the Tyneside apprentices' strike and then, a few weeks later, the four anarchists for Freedom Press publications.

The *War Commentary* trial ended on April 26th 1945. The four accused stood charged with conduct liable to prejudice recruitment to the armed forces. But by then the Second World War was on its last gasp. Germany surrendered unconditionally a fortnight later. Nothing any publication wrote could affect the ultimate outcome. Moreover, the big problem facing the British govern-ment was not to increase recruitment; rather it was to increase the speed of demobilisation.

So the intriguing question is: why did the State bother to continue pursuing the case? In my opinion, it deeply feared the armed forces turning its strength against the British ruling class. As another German – Karl Liebknecht – once said: "The enemy is at home".

Franco's Spain: Britain's Silent Friend

O n July 9th 1936, a De Havilland Rapide aircraft left Croydon airport. Aboard were two British intelligence officers. Ostensibly, they were supposed to be going on holiday. To improve their cover, two young ladies accompanied them. In fact, they flew to Morocco, where they picked up General Franco. They then went on to the Canaries. It was from there that Franco started his uprising against the democratically elected government of Spain.

It seems also certain that Major Hugh Pollard and Douglas Jerrold were carrying out the instructions of the Foreign Office rather than acting as private individuals. Official flies, recently opened, reveal that the Spanish generals informed the British government in advance of their intention to stage a coup d'etat. The provision of an aircraft to ferry Franco was merely a friendly gesture of goodwill by the British government. The military dictators were expected to be quickly victorious. Nobody anticipated, however, the De Havilland Rapide's flight would set the fuse alight to an exceptionally bloody three-year civil war.[1]

For some time before hostilities began in Spain, the British government had looked on in alarm at the growing disturbances and violence on the Iberian peninsular. It affected UK persons and property. British businessmen owned 40% of the foreign capital invested in Spain. Their capital dominated mining, electricity, railways and fruit growing. English shipping companies carried 40% of Spanish overseas trade.

---

1. Anthony Cave Brown and Charles B. MacDonald, *The Communist International and the Coming of World War Two*, London, 1981, pp. 424-5. Major Hugh Pollard, who had links with the Imperial General Staff, admitted flying Franco to the Canaries on a BBC 2 television series about the Spanish civil war. According to Professor Logie Barrow, of Bremen University, one of the two young women taken as passengers recounted her experiences in an article that appeared in *Readers' Digest* in the 1950s.

The rising tide of troubles inevitably spilled over on to British property. Workers occupied Richard Yeoward's banana plantation at Tenerife. Strikes happened at Rio Tinto Zinc's mines in Andalusia as well as the Zafra-Husho railway and elsewhere. In May 1936, a British businessman, the owner of a ceramics factory at Seville, was badly beaten up. On July 2nd, Michael Hood, head of a British textile firm in Barcelona, was killed. Portugal's dictator, General Salazar, wrote a private letter to the Foreign Office, warning that Spanish discontent was beginning to spill over into his country, destabilising the regime. Even more disturbing was a letter from Spain that the British prime minister, Stanley Baldwin, received from the distinguished historian Arthur Bryant: "In Spain things are far worse than is realised... the revolution is beginning".[1]

Quite understandably, British government was mightily worried. Besides the threat to British interests in Spain and Portugal, there was the problem of Gibraltar. Dependent on Spain for many things, the small colony would become indefensible against a hostile hinterland. Yet, Britain's interests in the Middle East, including oil, depended upon this vital lifeline. Likewise the quickest supply route to India and other British possessions in the Orient necessitated this militarily–strategic rock remaining British. Besides all this, British rulers feared that, should Spain's disorders be permitted to remain unchecked–indeed to worsen–then the virus of revolution might spread to other parts of Europe. A repeat of October 1917 might well be in the offing. Is it any wonder the British cabinet would rather see a dictatorship of General Franco than continued disorder and perhaps the prospect of a workers' government?

But the Baldwin, and later Chamberlain, administrations realistically recognised a constraint–the necessity of operating within the parameters of the politically possible. For example, it would be inconceivable for British troops to fight alongside their German and Italian counterparts, providing a sixth column to besiege Madrid. Nor could the RAF replace the Condor legion to terror-bomb the Basque town of Guernica. The British people, imbued with democratic tradition, would not countenance such conduct being done in its name. Widespread public anger would threaten the Tory government's very existence. Therefore, Whitehall mandarins devised a cunning ploy to attain the same aim while avoiding the hostility. The new policy was called non-intervention. It resembled a suggestion made by a character in a Cervantes story: he confidentially forecast he could solve, completely and permanently, all Spain's economic problems. His only proviso was that every Spaniard had got to stop eating for three months!

In the same way Britain's policy of non-intervention solved the problem of Spanish instability by starving the democratic government. Though superficially even-handed, it had a hidden agenda: the policy stopped the Republican side receiving supplies essential to its war effort while Nazi Germany and fascist Italy continued to equip Franco's armies with supplies essential to them.

---

1. Enrique Moradiellos, 'British Political Strategy in the Face of the Military Rising of 1936 in Spain', *Contemporary European History*, July 1992, provides a useful summary of the official British position.

THE SPANISH REVOLUTION FAILED

In these circumstances, the ultimate outcome of the war never remained in doubt. Nor, privately, did Britain's rulers envisage any other outcome. As Sir Robert Vansittart conceded in a private Foreign Office memo, written in January 1939: "the non-intervention policy has been putting a premium on Franco's victory".[1]

Actually, subsequent research reveals the term 'non-intervention' understates the position. Franco's death and the opening of Spanish archives reveal that British firms secretly backed the fascists during the civil war. Anglo-American oil fuelled Franco's aeroplanes and tanks. Companies like Rio Tinto Zinc provided him with the valuable sinews of war. Shipping materials from abroad did not always go smoothly: when the crew of SS Lmana berthed at Boston, Massachusetts, they discovered their next job was to ship materials vital to Franco's war effort to Spain All the men went on strike. Whereupon the British consul threatened them with prosecution under the Merchant Shipping Act, 1894 The crew, led by a Geordie militant named Spike Robson, stayed solid and prosecution ensued. At the Liverpool assizes, they faced a total of 85 charges, but finished up with a mere £2 fine each. On appeal, the court dismissed the employer's case, rescinded the £2 fine, and awarded costs to the crew. Spike Robson and his comrades had established an important legal principle: seamen

---

1. *Ibid.*

asked to take goods to a war zone, when this had not been part of the original terms of employment, could refuse to obey.[1]

Once the civil war ended and the new dictatorship had been installed, profit-able trade resumed without any such legal impediment. Franco needed eco-nomic help from Britain, France and the United States to repair the ravages of three years' conflict. This was forthcoming, even after the Second World War broke out. Churchill assured Franco that the Royal Navy would not blockade Spain; it would supply Spain with goods desperately needed for reconstruc-tion. In return, Franco provided valuable raw materials (mercury, zinc, lead, etc.) that were vital to the Allies' struggle against Germany. He also refused to permit German troops to enter his country. As a consequence, Gibraltar stayed securely in British hands, the supply lines to the Middle East still open. Had the Wehrmacht been able to shut the Mediterranean to Allied shipping, Rom-mel and his panzer divisions would have captured Egypt and probably gone on to the oilfields of the Middle East. Gibraltar's loss would also have forced British shipping to use the circuitous route round the Cape, a much longer and more expensive journey that would have seriously handicapped the fight against Japan.

Willard L. Beaulac's book, aptly titled *Franco: Silent Ally in World War Two*, gives an admirably full account of this mutual assistance.[2] As he worked as a high-ranking United States official at the American embassy in Madrid, he was ideally placed to gain a firsthand – as well as an underhand – view of these sordid transactions.

But Beaulac's book fails to deal with British Labour leaders' complicity in maintaining Franco's cruel regime, a role similar to that of the Stalinists in se-curing Franco's triumph in the first place. When he became Churchill's deputy prime minister, Attlee completely forgot the verbal support he had given Re-publican Spain a few years previously. At the 1937 Labour Party Conference, Attlee had created an emotional scene: delegates' cheered as he held aloft the arm of Spain's prime minister, Juan Negrin, in a gesture of solidarity. Yet, three years' later, when Franco hinted he regarded it an unfriendly act for Britain to provide Negrin with a refuge in this country, Attlee immediately resolved to send the Spanish politician packing. He told him to go to South America or New Zealand. When news of this became public, an outcry arose from the labour movement. Emrys Hughes, in the independent socialist weekly, *Forward*, made a vitriolic onslaught on Attlee's lack of principles, particularly socialist

---

1. The pamphlet, 'Spike Robson: class fighter', published by North Tyneside Trades Council in 1987, gives an account on pp. 10–1. Also, Nigel Todd, *In Excited Times: The People Against the Blackshirts*, (Whitley Bay, 1994) p. 99.
2. Willard L. Beaulac, *Franco: Silent Ally in World War Two*, South Illinois University Press, 1985.

ones.[1] Under intense pressure, Attlee partially relented: Negrin could remain in Britain so long as he did not make any anti-Franco utterances.[2]

Worse happened three years later. After the Allies so-called 'liberation' of North Africa, Spanish republicans in Algeria, who had fled there after fighting against Franco in the civil war, expected better treatment than they had been getting from their pro-Nazi captors. But the American and British occupying authorities kept the same Vichy colonial rulers in charge as there had been before. Franco would have been annoyed if conditions had been improved for his enemies. So thousands of hapless Spaniards continued to work on chain gangs, building the Trans-Saharan railway from Colom-Bechar to Bon-Arfan. Their pay was half a franc a day. Punishment for not doing the allotted work stint was imprisonment in a detention camp 400 miles in the desert, a kind of Saharan equivalent to Devil's island.[3]

In Britain, ex-Spanish Republican soldiers fared only slightly better. They were treated rather like common criminals. In 1945, the British left mounted a campaign because 500 Spanish ex-Republican soldiers were detained in a prisoner-of-war camp at Kirkham in Lancashire. Presumably, because the authorities believed fascists and anti-fascists mixed happily together, the majority of the camp inmates were German and Italian POWs. Though enemy soldiers could return home after hostilities had ended, this option was not open to Spaniards. They remained behind bars. A protest meeting, chaired by Fenner Brockway and with George Orwell as the main speaker, was held at Holborn Hall,

London, on March 26th 1946. Leaflets advertising the meeting read 'Do you support Franco? If not, demand the release of Spanish Republicans imprisoned in England'. Among those backing the campaigns were well-known figures like Benjamin Britten, E.M. Forster, Herbert Read and Osbert Sitwell. Yet, according to the *Socialist Leader*, at least 180 Spaniards were still being incarcerated by the Attlee administration in 1948.[4]

Consistent with its pro-Franco line, the Labour government remained hostile to refugees fleeing Spain. When 136 men and women managed to escape and arrived at British ports, the authorities said their entry was illegal and they had no papers. Therefore, they were sent back to probable torture and death. At

---

1. *Forward*, November 30th, 1940.
2. Claud Cockburn first leaked the story of Negrin's impending eviction from England in *The Week*. It was then taken up in the *Forward*, November 30th, 1940, and other radical journals. Even when the Second World War was drawing to a close, the Foreign Office refused to relax the ban. *The Daily Worker*, of January 3rd, 1945, reported it had refused to permit Negrin to send a recorded message to an anti-Franco meeting to be held in New York.
3. *Forward*, May 1st, 1943. Lead article headlined 'Forgotten Men: Tragedy of Spanish Anti-Fascists'.
4. *Socialist Leader*, September 10th, 1948. Leaflets were published by the Freedom Defence Committee. Roy Marsden of Barlow Moor Road, Manchester has transcripts of three anti-fascist Spaniards who underwent the ordeal of imprisonment by the Labour government.

NIGHT ATTACK ON THE ARAGON FRONT

THE WHOLE OF THIS STORY IS IN THE WORDS OF THE MEN WHO TOOK PART IN IT. IT CONSISTS ENTIRELY OF EXTRACTS FROM LETTERS TO JOHN McNAIR FROM BOB SMILLIE, ERIC BLAIR, ALBERT GROSS AND PADDY DONOVAN.

A Spanish comrade rose and rushed forward. "Por cllos — Arriba! (For the others—charge!) "Charge!" shouted Blair. "Over to the right and in" called Paddy Donovan. "Are we downhearted?" cried the French Captain Benjamin.

In front of the parapet was Eric Blair's tall figure coolly strolling forward through the storm of fire. He leapt at the parapet, then stumbled. Hell, had they got him? No, he was over, closely followed by Gross, of Hammersmith, Frankfort, of Hackney, and Bob Smillie, with the others right after them.

The trench had been hastily evacuated. The last of the retreating Fascists, clothed only in a blanket, was thirty yards away. Blair gave chase, but the man threw the ground

FORWARD!

I was a dirty night. Rain was

BOB SMILLIE

give the impression we were a thousand instead of ten.

"They're coming back!" Over went a bomb. The explosion was fol-

BOB EDWARDS
Leader of the
I.L.P.
Contingent

TRIBUTE

FROM GEORGE KOPP, COMMANDER OF THE 3rd REGIMENT, DIVISION LENIN, P.O.U.M.

WE have had a very hot time here these last days, and have advanced some thousand yards. The enemy counter-attacked, but did not succeed in regaining an inch of the lost ground. On the night of the 13th we made a somewhat audacious raid on the enemy's positions near the Ermita Salas in order to relieve pres-

with the diplomatic list of national dictators and ambassadors.

At the present moment we, the workers of the world are winning on all fronts. The battles are bloody, the casualties are many.

This struggle is also your struggle. Are you doing your part? The help we most need finds its mark in the way of medical supplies. You can do your part by sending your financial assistance to the I.L.P. Offices, 35 St. Bride Street, London, E.C.4. The cost of medical supplies for the workers will go there real. However small or however great it be, send your donation now.

Viva la Revolucion! On to Workers Control!

[These extracts are from Paul Porter, member of the I.L.P. Contingent, who is now living in Australia in Barcelona, having been wounded some days before the attack described on this Page.]

FRANK FRANKFORD

Our objective was a Fascist parapet which dominated our lines. The plan was as follows:—we were to creep up, cut the wire, all three, our bombs at an agreed signal, and then rush the parapet. Meanwhile the shock troops were to assault another position in the rear of ours to prevent a counter-attack from that side. Our part of the job worked more or less according to plan.

★

We crawled forward in single file through pools of water into ditches which soaked us up to the thighs, through fields, cutting barbed wire as we went. Visibility was almost nil. We got within about thirty yards of the enemy, and could hear two sentries chatting together quietly. Then with a red spear of flame, a sentry's rifle went off. Jorge rose up and flung the first bomb. "Bombs!!" Over they went. Hell started. On our left a machine gun opened on us, rifles spattered a stream of bullets over our head. A few yards in front a bomb burst with a roar and a sheet of flame and sparks like a gigantic firework display. More bombs exploded around us. We began to wriggle back a bit. Thomas called out, "I'm hit." Thompson, too, said, "I've caught one." "Go back," we said, but he refused.

C. JUSTESEN

trench was one dead man: in a dugout was another body.

We looked around quickly, less than a dozen of us. We had got them out. Now to hold the position. There was already the beginning of a counter-attack in our rear. Guns were jammed with the mud we had been through. Only six or seven rifles were working, with them we began, turning support fire on our side. In the other, where there was an unprotected gap, we took sandbags from the parapet to build a small barricade behind which three or four men could lie down and fire. We had used up most of our bombs. We had captured a quantity of Fascist bombs, but these were of a different make from ours, and we were not certain how to use them.

"Viva P.O.U.M.!" we yelled, trying to gather reinforcements, and to

★

HUGH McNEILL

and I can sit fire.

O'Hara, among the first to reach the parapet, left it again to bandage up two rather comrades who were fixing our sonder fire. With great bravery and coolness he achieved this difficult task.

"Give me a Mauser," said Tanky.

"Mr Worcester's jammed."

"Anybody else need bandaging?" yells O'Hara.

"Here's a telescope," said Moyle.

So an hour compressed itself into a few fleeting impressions.

Soon it became evident that the parapet on our left had not been taken. From three sides we were assailed by a hurricane of machine-gun and rifle fire, mortar and artillery had started, and we were in for a tough time. The Fascists were closing in. It was obvious that we should have to clear our soon. Benjamin gave the order to retire. Reluctantly we retreated through the

STAFFORD COTTMANN

REG. HIDDLESTONE

twas fire in our own lines, taking an hours 2,000 rounds of ammunition and some bombs.

When we got to Jorge Hiddlestone and Cole were missing. They did not appear until about an hour later. Jorge was hit through the shoulder. Hiddlestone was was badly shattered and Cole had stayed to help Hiddlestone in.

Our boys of the guard did I.L.P. did their job and dam'n well. With dow, English boys, said the Spanish Captain Jorge. Tonight we are going out to get a box of bombs we had to leave in no man's land.

PHILIP HUNTER

The ILP contingent's attack was led by Eric Blair, who became better known as George Orwell.

one port six desperate Spaniards jumped overboard. This did not save them. It merely meant they met their fates more rapidly: their return was made by aircraft.[1]

In the much bigger and more fundamental level, however, the British Labour government stands exposed by the way it gave aid and succour to Franco after 1945. Without this help his tyrannical regime would have been unable to survive. The economies of virtually every other country had been wrecked by the war; almost all Spain's foreign trade had to be with the two countries – Britain and the United States – where relative normality remained. This placed the Attlee administration in an exceedingly strong position. By imposing an economic boycott, the Spanish dictatorship would quickly have collapsed. Yet, Labour failed to lift its little finger to topple Franco.

Another course of action would have been equally effective. In 1944, as the Allied troops advanced in France, the military high command was glad to see a sizeable section of the French resistance movement preoccupied with fighting much better equipped German forces in the ports along the Bay of Biscay. In that way their energies were frittered away; they were kept from Paris, the place where the decisive question of political power would be decided and where armed workers could have had a far bigger say – perhaps a decisive say – in the ultimate outcome.

Even so, resistance fighters could still have won a subsidiary prize. After vanquishing the Wehrmacht at Bordeaux and elsewhere, a lot of them thought that the logical next step would be – if it really had been a war for democracy – to continue by going over the Pyrenees to finish the Franco dictatorship off as well. Many French people have close links with Spaniards, particularly from the Basque region. Indeed, some Spanish refugees had fought in the French resistance. So why should they not repay a debt of honour? In 1945-1947, a number of attempts were made to overthrow Franco by building a popular resistance movement. But both the French and British governments frowned on such schemes. They would far rather let the Spanish people suffer under a savage dictator than risk the de-stabilisation of the Iberian peninsular, a mass revolt that might spread to other parts of the Continent.

The Franco regime was allowed to fester on until he eventually died of natural causes. Besides imposing an immense burden of suffering on the entire Spanish people, those most especially affected were the political refugees, condemned to struggle to make a living in a foreign land, far away from their families and friends. Books like Louis Stein's *Beyond Death and Exile* and Nancy MacDonald's *Homage to the Spanish Exiles* give some idea of the pain these unfortunate people had to endure.[2] Some were anarchists, others were Trotskyists or members of the POUM, the majority were just ordinary anti-fascist workers and peasants.

---

1. Louis Stern, *Beyond Death and Exile*, Harvard, 1979, pp. 257-9.

2. Nancy MacDonald's *Homage to the Spanish Exiles*, New York: Insight Books, 1987.

Not only were the Stalinists, by drowning the Spanish revolution in blood, responsible for all this agony, the labour lieutenants of capitalism also stand in the dock condemned.

'Hallo! Hallo! Art Department? Who the ******* hell got those photographs mixed up?'

The Origins of the Cold War

An entire generation has grown up amid the Cold War, with the threat of nuclear holocaust ever-present. It therefore becomes highly apposite to ask two questions. How did it start? What were international relations like before it began? Some well-meaning people, believing that the ending of the Cold War has overriding importance, look back with nostalgia to the time when Britain, the United States and Russia lived in friendship with each other. They seek to end the Cold War without fundamentally altering existing political systems. They do not realise that the present international tension is the product of rival imperialisms, of state capitalism in Russia and monopoly capitalism in America. Rather these misguided people see the conflict in facile terms, as a consequence of misunderstandings, and believed that all would be well if these could be eliminated.

Of course, it is an illusion to believe that understanding necessarily leads to agreement. The more fully we understand the capitalist system, the more implacable our hostility becomes. But it is also equally wrong to regard the period of East-West friendship as some kind of bygone golden age; it was much more another kind of hell.

In his fine book, *The Politics of War*, Professor Kolko describes the cordial atmosphere that prevailed at the Yalta conference just 25 years ago:

> *The dinner meetings were often extremely cordial and personally friendly, so much so that Stalin and Churchill uttered effusive words equal to the occasions again and again, with Roosevelt making plainer, less eloquent homilies by virtue of his more limited oratorical talents, but also imbibing the atmosphere of goodwill. Churchill, who had fought Bolshevism everywhere and had in prior weeks advocated the suppression of the Left by bullets and blood, could now talk of 'Stalin's life as most precious to the hopes and hearts of all of us', pledging 'We shall not weaken in supporting your exertions'. Stalin could reply in kind, even more expansively, toasting 'In the history of diplomacy I know of no such*

> close alliance of three Great Powers as this... an alliance for lasting peace... the
> atmosphere at this dinner was as that of a family, like the relations between our
> countries' the less verbally agile Roosevelt could chime.[1]

The alliance between America, Britain and Russia rested on shared objectives.
The Axis threatened their vital economic and political interests. Consequently,
they all had a common concern to defeat it. Moreover, once the Axis was vanquished, they could enjoy the spoils of victory – in other words, their unity was
based on the cohesive power of impending plunder.

Allied statesmen were singularly uninhibited about expressing themselves in
terms of power politics. Churchill described the Big Three as a "very exclusive
club", where the entrance fee was "at least five million soldiers or the equivalent". Stalin appears not to have uttered the remark so often attributed to
him – "The Pope? How many divisions has he got?" – but he nevertheless believed that military might should be the supreme political arbiter. At the second
Yalta plenum session, he said France's views should be disregarded since she
"had only eight divisions in the war". Despite mounting democratic platitudes,
Roosevelt likewise concurred with the opinion that the powerful few should
dictate to the rest of the world. He declared "that the peace should be written
by the three powers represented at this table". To which Churchill added: "The
eagle should permit the small birds to sing and care not wherefore they sang".

Capitalist politicians often talk about defending the smaller nations from attack. It gives an idealistic tinge to their sordid dealings. Britain's declaration
of war against Germany in 1939 was ostensibly because of Hitler's invasion
of Poland. In fact, the underlying reason was to protect the extensive investments of British businessmen in the Balkans, wealth that was becoming more
and more vulnerable as a result of Germany's *Dracht nach Osten* – the drive to
the East. Likewise today, NATO politicians suddenly feel obliged to refer the
importance of the independence of small countries when Russia violates them,
such as the suppression of the Hungarian uprising in 1956 and the military occupation of Czechoslovakia in 1968. What nauseating hypocrisy this all is was
exposed in the 'peace' negotiations: the Big Three did not spare a thought for
the right of peoples to self-determination and national independence.

In The Thieves' Kitchen

Something of the contempt with which small nations were treated can be gath-
ered from Churchill's own account of how he reached agreement with Stalin,
at Moscow in October 1944, about the Balkans:

> *The moment was apt for business, so I said, 'Let us settle about our affairs in
> the Balkans. Your armies are in Rumania and Bulgaria. We have interests,
> missions and agents there. Don't let us get at cross-purposes in small ways. So
> far as Britain and Russia are concerned, how would it do for you to have 90%
> predominance in Rumania, for us to have 90% of the say in Greece, and go*

1. Gabriel Kolko, *The Politics of War*, Random House, 1968, p. 367.

50-50 about Yugoslavia?' While this was being translated, I wrote on a half-sheet of paper:

Rumania	
Russia	90%
The others	10%
Greece	
Great Britain	90%
Russia	10%
Yugoslavia	50-50%
Hungary	50-50%
Bulgaria	
Russia	75%
The others	25%

I pushed this across to Stalin, who had by then heard the translation. There was a slight pause. Then he took his blue pencil and made a large tick upon it, and passed it back to us. It was all settled in no more time than it takes to set down...

After this there was a long silence. The pencilled paper lay on the centre of the table. At length I said, 'Might it not be thought rather cynical if it seemed we had disposed of these issues, so fateful to millions of people, in such an offhand manner? Let us burn the paper'.

'No, you keep it' said Stalin.[1]

In the disregard they showed for human life and values, the Big Three displayed a barbaric depravity reminiscent of the worst of the Roman emperors. For example, at the Teheran conference in 1944, Stalin, whose path to power in Russia had been along a trail of blood, moved a toast to "the death of at least 50,000 German officers". Roosevelt thought this an excellent idea. But Churchill refused to drink, saying "Great Britain could never admit the killing of prisoners of war". This led to a slight quarrel. However, no such disagreement arose at the Yalta conference:

The President said that he had been very much struck by the extent of German destruction in the Crimea and therefore he was more bloodthirsty in regard to the Germans than he had been a year ago. And he hoped that Marshal Stalin would again propose a toast to the execution of 50,000 officers of the German army.

Marshal Stalin replied that everyone was more bloodthirsty than they had been a year ago... He said the Germans were savages and seemed to hate with a sadistic hatred the creative work of human beings.

The President agreed with this.[2]

---

1. Winston Churchill, *Second World War, Vol VI*, p. 1983; J. Ciechanowski, *Defeat in Victory*, pp. 292-3.
2. W. Bohlen's account, cited by Hal Draper, *Behind Yalta: The Truth About the War*, in *Labor Action*, April 4th, 1955

Then the Big Three drank their ghoulish toast. Later, Roosevelt's chief adviser, Harry Hopkins, admitted to Stalin "he looked forward to what for him would be a pleasant spectacle, the present state of Berlin—and he might even be able to find Hitler's body".[1]

In such a frame of mind, Allied leaders could contemplate mass murder of both soldiers and civilians with equanimity. This was clearly revealed when they came to discuss the fate of Silesia and East Prussia at the fourth Yalta plenary session. Stalin said there would be no problem since the Germans fled from those regions before the oncoming Red Army. Churchill then replied that this was only a partial solution since they had simply fled into the heartland of Germany and would have to be handled there:

> 'We have killed six or seven million' Churchill continued, 'and probably will kill
> another million before the end of the war'. 'One or two?' asked Stalin.
> 'Oh, I am not proposing any limitation on them,' replied Churchill.

The Allied statesmen watched the collapse of Germany like vultures, ready to grab any tender morsels. Stalin wanted to take German factories to be reassembled in Russia. He also wanted millions of German workers used as forced labour in Russia. This method of rebuilding the battered economy of USSR neatly fitted in with the interests of British capitalism: Churchill made it plain that, while Russia grabbed German factories and workers, Britain would be free to snatch Germany's export markets. So the alliance rested upon a confluence of exploitative interests.

Behind this lay an even greater kinship of interests: the desire to crush revolutionary forces that were emerging in every country as the war drew to a close. The Big Three were conscious that the Old Order was very vulnerable. In Germany the capitalist class—particularly the big capitalists like Krupps, I G Farben and Thyssen—had supported fascism financially and in every other way. In other European countries under German occupation, the ruling classes had reached a detente with Hitler. They discovered that it was not only prudent but profitable to support the Nazis war effort. This meant they had become politically discredited, completely alienated from the rest of the population. At the same time, the majority of the people in these countries wanted to see new societies built after the war, not reconstruction along the old lines. What made things even more dangerous, many of them were not merely left-wingers but also armed and disciplined members of resistance movements.

In these circumstances, the Big Three found the restoration of bourgeois society a difficult, delicate operation. For, with greater justification than when Marx first uttered it in 1848, it could be said, "A spectre is haunting Europe—it is the spectre of communism". Fortunately for the various ruling classes, capitalism found its saviour in Joseph Stalin—a man who already possessed great experience at exterminating Bolsheviks.

---

1. Robert Sherwood, *Roosevelt and Hopkins: An Intimate History*, Enigma Books, p. 912.

It is interesting to compare Stalin's role with that of Lenin after the First World War. While Stalin praised the decisions taken at Yalta, Lenin attacked those of Versailles:

> *We see a monstrous intensification of oppression. We see a reversion to colonial and military oppression far worse than that which existed before. The Versailles Treaty has put Germany and a number of other vanquished countries in conditions in which economic existence is materially impossible, in conditions of utter lack of rights and degradation.*[1]

Lenin denounced "the thieves' kitchen" in 1919; Stalin was one of the main thieves in 1945. Differences did not end there. Lenin was deeply imbued with the spirit of socialist internationalism whereas Stalin had nationalist prejudices. Frequently, in his speeches, Stalin would utter racist remarks, such as "the Germans are savages" or the Poles are "quarrelsome". It is obvious he did not believe that, as the *Communist Manifesto* said, workers have no fatherland. Such sentiments were alien to Stalin, who pressed the claims of the Kremlin bureaucracy for fresh territory in Tsarist terms. He wanted slices of northern China because, he told Roosevelt, they belonged to Russia before the Russo-Japanese war of 1904-1905. He introduced his own draft of the agreement at Yalta on February 8th, 1945, with the following reactionary preamble: "The former rights of Russia violated by the treacherous attack of Japan in 1904 should be restored". He went on to justify the grabbing of the Manchurian railway with the argument that "the tsars had use of the line".[2] Stalin's inspiration came from the Romanov dynasty rather than from revolution.

Lenin made it clear his attitude was totally different:

> *My task, the task of a representative of the revolutionary proletariat, is to prepare the* world proletarian revolution *as the* only *salvation from the horrors of world war. I have to reason not from the point of view of 'my' country... but from the point of view of my participation in preparing, preaching and hastening the world proletarian revolution.*[3]

This policy of Lenin was the exact opposite of Stalin's policy in 1945, and the reason for this must be sought in Russia's internal regime. By a series of measures in the twenties and thirties, the Kremlin bureaucracy had installed itself as the ruling class of a state capitalist society.[4] If, at the end of the Second World War revolution broke out in any part of Europe, it might easily spread and endanger the Stalinist regime in Russia. Therefore, the Kremlin had a vested interest in trying to maintain the status quo. A further advantage that might arise for Stalin from such a policy: by playing a counter-revolutionary role – in other words, helping the United States and Britain to make capitalism secure in Europe – he was likely to endear himself to them. In turn, America and Britain

---

1. V. I. Lenin, *Selected Works, vol x*, p. 182.
2. R. Sherwood, op. cit., p. 866.
3. V. I. Lenin, *Selected Works, vol vii*, p. 177. Emphasis in original.
4. G. Kolko, op. cit., p. 165.

might reciprocate and show their goodwill by letting the Russian rulers plunder defeated Germany even more viciously.

Holding Off Revolution

In the grand design of the Kremlin, its obedient servants – the Communist Parties in the various countries – had a vital part to play. As Professor Kolko rightly remarks, "the Communists throughout Europe inhibited decisive action by the local leftists, giving the Old Order a breathing spell". He continues by saying:

> *If the Russians had not given the West a respite, in fact Washington may have realised its worst fears everywhere in 1945. For only Russian conservatism stood between the Old Order and the revolution.*[1]

Professor Kolko proves this thesis with a wealth of factual material, which makes his book extremely valuable. Let me cite some of it:

Italy

In 1943, Marshal Badoglio, the fascist general who had led Mussolini's invasion of Abysinnia, is placed head of the provisional government in that part of the country occupied by Allied troops. Both Badoglio and the king, Victor Emmanuel, "were universally regarded as remnants of the equally widely hated fascist order",[2] yet the Russian government recognised this regime and called upon the Italian people to support a coalition government under Badoglio's leadership,[3] The Italian Communist Party obeyed this instruction, and Badoglio praised Togliatti as "the most effective collaborator".[4] This cooperation was given despite the fact that "many anti-fascists were still in prison"[5] and that Badoglio's government "strongly opposed any serious dismissal of the fascists".[6] Liberals like Sforza "and the Socialists under Pietro Nenni were consistently more troublesome than the Communist party. For one thing, they were not under Moscow discipline, which was now a moderating factor".[7]

France

The large and influential French Communist Party:

---

1. *Ibid.*
2. *Ibid*, p.46.
3. *Ibid*, p.52.
4. *Ibid*, p.54.
5. *Ibid*, p.56.
6. *Ibid*, p.57.
7. *Ibid*, p.55.

helped to disarm the Resistance, revive a moribund economy, and create suf-ficient stability to give the Old Order a crucial breathing spell – and later took much pride in its accomplishment.[1]

The unity of the nation, Thorez never tired of reiterating, was a categorical imperative.[2]

CPers joined a coalition government under De Gaulle's leadership. As a min-ister, Thorez "banned strikes, demanded more labour from the workers, and endorsed the dissolution of the Free French Forces".[3] He even urged "min-ers to send their wives and daughters into the pits to increase production",[4] "De Gaulle appreciated Thorez".[5] Foreign Minister George Bidault assured the Americans he was "the best of the lot".[6] On colonialism, the French CPers' stance "was for all practical purposes one of 'Progressive Empire' and at no time did they advocate immediate colonial independence".[7] "During mid-1945 the Communists severely condemned the first post-war stirring of the inde-pendence movement against French control in Algeria as 'fascist' uprisings'".[8] Communist Party members were in the government that sent troops to Indo-China to restore French colonial rule and fight against Ho Chi Minh.

Professor Kolko does not deal with the British Communist Party, which has always been small and insignificant. Nevertheless, it is interesting to examine its role. In industry, communists led the speed-up campaign, broke strikes and called for the victimisation of militants. The Communist Party supported Con-servative candidates in parliamentary by-elections.[9] Not merely the Trotskyists but also Socialists like James Maxton, MP, and Fenner (later Lord) Brockway were described as "Hitler's agents".[10] A Communist Party pamphlet recom-mended:

> *Expose every Trotskyist you come into contact with. Show other people where his ideas are leading. Treat him as you would treat an open Nazi.*

---

1. *Ibid*, p.95.
2. *Ibid.*
3. *Ibid.*
4. *Ibid*, p.444.
5. *Ibid*, p.94.
6. *Ibid.*
7. *Ibid*, p.442.
8. *Ibid*, p.443.
9. If I may be permitted a personal footnote, I came into politics as a result of the Lancaster by-election of October 1941. Communist Party members smashed an ILP election meeting and then went to offer their help to Brigadier-General MacLean, the Conservative candidate.
10. W. Wainwright's pamphlet, *Clear Out Hitler's Agents*, published by the Communist Party, August 1942. 'A vote for Brockway is a vote for Hitler' was used by the CP when Brockway stood as an ILP candidate at Cardiff in 1942, and at Lancaster the previous year.

In other words, this was a clear incitement to use violence against the Left. At the same time, the Communist Party displayed affection towards the Right. In his history of the Communist Party, Professor Pelling tells how, as the 1945 general election approached, the party called for a peacetime coalition government:

> (Pollitt said that) there should be a 'new National Government' which should include 'representatives of all parties supporting the decisions of the Crimea Conference'. Believing that Winston Churchill, with all the prestige of an architect of victory, would be invincible at the polls, the party favoured the maintenance of the coalition at the end of the war – or as Dutt put it, 'the firm united stand of the majority supporters of Crimea in all the principal parties'... Unfortunately for the Communists, the Labour Party leaders were in no mood for a coalition having decided, with a shrewder sense of political realities, that they stood a good chance of winning an election as an independent force.[1]

The Communist Party's policy at the 1945 general election had strange repercussions the following year, when the party applied for affiliation to the Labour Party. At the 1946 Labour conference, Herbert Morrison, speaking for the national executive, advised delegates to reject the resolution. With delightful irony, Morrison showed that the Labour Party's line had, at the general election, been far to the left of the Communists, who had advocated a:

> policy which was inconsistent with the principles either of Karl Marx, the doctrines of class consciousness, or the doctrines of class struggle'.

He continued:

> Behind this policy for the General Election there was, first of all, a belief that Labour could not get a clear parliamentary majority. That was defeatism, just before the election began.

Morrison castigated them for advocating:

> a policy of full co-operation with capitalism and a complete desertion of socialist principles... They are not a Party of the Left as far as I can see.[2]

That a Labour leader like Morrison, an extreme right-winger, could adopt a political position to the left of the Communist Party merely indicates how right-wing the Communist Party happened to be. The same situation prevailed throughout the world: wherever possible, the Communist Party's attempted to direct popular forces into channels that were harmless to the ruling class. But to this general pattern, there appears to have been three kinds of deviation.

---

1. Henry Pelling, *The British Communist Party*, pp.130-1.
2. Report of the 45th annual conference of the Labour Party, Bournemouth, 1946, pp. 170-1.

The Exceptions

First, where the Communist Parties entirely owed their power and influence to their own exertions and were therefore in a position where they could disregard the conservative Moscow line (e.g., in Yugoslavia). Second, where the Communist Party was too small and the Resistance Movement too large for the Communist Party to control it (e.g., in Greece). Third, where the society was in such an advanced state of degeneration that it was in practice impossible for the Communist Party, to maintain the status quo (e.g., in China).

Let us analyse these three situations in turn.

1) After the German invasion of Yugoslavia in 1941, a three-sided conflict developed. There were the Chetnik guerrillas, led by Mihailovic, who wanted to restore the reactionary monarchy Then there were the partisans, led by Tito, only about 5% of whose membership were initially communists. These two resistance movements became openly hostile to each other – indeed, probably fought more among themselves than with the German invader – because Mihailovic realised that, if Tito's partisans gained large popular support, they would constitute a serious (and armed) threat to the restoration of King Peter's monarchical despotism. Tito and his comrades also represented a long-term threat to the Russian bureaucracy since their growing popularity came from appealing to pan-Slav nationalism, federal principles and national equality, ideas which were at variance with the Kremlin's desire to extend its influence throughout the Balkans.

The Russian leaders showed their displeasure with Tito's partisans. They recognised King Peter as the rightful ruler of Yugoslavia. They refused to read Tito's proclamations over Moscow radio. They even sent a Russian military mission in 1943 and military aid to Mihailovic. It was during this period that a telegram which Stalin received from the Partisans began, "If you cannot send us assistance, then at least do not hamper us" profoundly shaped his impression of Tito. Georgi Dimitrov, the leading Bulgarian communist, reported that Stalin "stamped with rage".[1]

Nevertheless, despite Stalin's disapproval, the Yugoslav partisans succeeded, largely by their own efforts, in expelling German troops from their country. This achievement, which was accomplished at immense human cost, was nothing less than miraculous: it is not generally known that the Yugoslav partisans kept more German and Italian divisions engaged than the Allies did in North

---

1. Vladimir Dedijer, *Tito*, p.232. Also Milovan Djilas, *Conversations with Stalin.*

Africa, nor that they killed 477,000 German and Italian soldiers and took 559,434 prisoner.[1]

After making such tremendous sacrifices, the Yugoslav partisans were in no mood to accept orders from Moscow. They were not prepared to see the Humpty-Dumpty-like figure of King Peter reinstalled in his Belgrade palace again. Stalin's orders were disobeyed.

2) In Greece, too, the resistance movement already had considerable power before British troops arrived. The National Liberation Front (EAM), a coalition of six political parties, had created the People's Liberation Army (ELAS) in 1942 to combine the armed and political struggle.

Professor Kolko gives some idea of their success:

> By liberation the EAMS labour organisation controlled the entire working class, and it helped lead strikes in occupied territories throughout the war; the EAM itself administered two-thirds to four-fifths of Greece and claimed one and a half million members out of a total population only five times that figure – a claim, even if exaggerated, that probably was not far from the unknown truth.[2]

Professor Kolko continues:

> Of all the groups in the EAM, the Communists were the most willing to submerge social objectives to the needs of a United Front and the only group willing to explicitly designate Greece, as early as 1943, as part of the general British sphere of influence after the war.[3]

But the Greek Communist Party (KKE) had only a small membership and were unable to direct EAM in the way they wished. For the Greek people had good reason to hate British capitalism and fight against it again dominating their economy. Thraldom to Britain began early in the 19th century. By the end of the War of Independence in 1821, Greece owed British bankers £5m, though she had only borrowed one-third of that amount. Between 1825 and 1898 Greek governments borrowed 140 million from London banks, although she only received a small fraction of that figure. By 1945 all loans had been paid for sevenfold (interest, carrying charges, etc.), but still none of the principal had been paid off. By 1935, Greece was setting aside one-third of her total income for servicing these loans. Even during the depression of the thirties, British bankers compelled Greece to pay interest in gold in spite of the fact that

1. Ygael Gluckstein, *Stalin's Satellites in Europe*, p. 238. Ygael Gluckstein (20th May 1917-9th May 2000), aka Tony Cliff, developed a State Capitalist theory of Russia, originally in a duplicated internal document of the British RCP entitled *The Class Nature of Russia* (June 1948), later published as *Stalinist Russia. A Marxist Analysis* (1955), and later, in an expanded verison, as *State Capitalism in Russia* (1974). He was responsible for founding the Socialist Review Group in 1950, which would go on to become the Socialist Workers Party.

2. G. Kolko, op. cit., p. 173.

3. *Ibid.*

Britain itself was off the gold standard. A neo-colonial situation accompanied this economic domination, as Hal Draper, an American socialist, described:

> *The money that the Greek government did receive from the loans went largely into maintaining an army and navy, which served as a British adjunct. The poverty-stricken people of Greece were the slaves and bondsmen of British capital.[1]*

In 1945, Britain was as determined to reassert its control as the Greek people were to prevent this happening. Sixty thousand British troops, under General Scobie, fought with ELAS to re-establish the Old Order. When ELAS laid down their weapons, savage repression ensued:

> *There was casual terror of random assassinations and beatings, the systematic repression by security committee and court-martial that simply arrested EAM supporters and detained them without trial. The government tightly controlled trade unions, and charged former EAM underground government tax collectors with robbery and looting... When the British Parliamentary Legal Mission visited Greece at the end of the year they reported there was a minimum of 50,000 prisoners.[2]*

The British authorities used Royalists and fascists in their reign of terror. As Professor Kolko points out, Stalin remained loyal to British capitalism:

> *No one heard a word of reproach of British policy in Greece from the Soviet Union throughout this bloody period and Churchill appreciated it.*

When, in January 1945, Churchill tried to justify the Allies armed intervention in Greece, he told Parliament that British troops were there to prevent a situation:

> *in which all forms of Government would have been swept away, and naked, triumphant Trotskyism installed. I think Trotskyism is a better definition of Greek Communism and certain other sects than the normal word. It has the advantage of being equally hated in Russia.[3]*

Churchill used the term 'Trotskyist' very loosely to denote organisations that (i) were not amenable to Moscow's control and (ii) threatened British interests. He displayed the same inexactitude over 'Bolshevism', as Kolko shows:

> *When the Russians did send a mission to Tito, Churchill relates, they discouraged the introduction of Bolshevism in Yugoslavia.[4]*

---

1. Hal Draper's article in *Labor Action*, April 4th, 1955.
2. G. Kolko, op. cit., p.430. David Horowitz, in *From Yalta to Vietnam*, p. 65, says that the Greek government spent half its budget on the army and police and only 6% on reconstruction.
3. House of Commons debate, December 9th, 1944.
4. G. Kolko, op. cit., p. 153.

3)The corruption and chaos in China in 1945 beggars description. Perhaps the venality of Chiang Kai-Shek and his Kuomintang warlords is best shown by a few facts:

• By 1944, an American-made tyre cost 1,000 dollars and a spark-plug 75 dollars in Chungking.

• It cost US military forces eight to ten times the cost to service units in China compared to what it would cost in the United States.

• Chinese generals discovered their troops were a greater asset dead than alive; if alive, the generals could only steal half their meagre rations; dead, the generals could steal the entirety.[1]

Henry Morgenthau, Secretary to the US Treasury, described Chiang Kai-Shek's clique as "just a bunch of crooks". General Stilwell, an American adviser in China, shared this view; as did his successor Wedemeyer.[2] Despite such criticism and the tremendous cost, the United States was determined to back Chiang Kai-Shek to the utmost. It did this, first, because it saw that China was potentially a good market for US exports once the war had ended. Secondly, because the lavish aid made Chiang's clique a stooge government, which would do whatever the USA ordered. The United States bought for itself an extra vote in the 'peace' negotiations.

   The Kremlin rulers, simply concerned with their interests as a ruling class, were prepared to support Chiang Kai-Shek irrespective of the consequences for Mao Tse-tung. This had clearly been shown in an earlier period, when Japanese victories over Chiang threatened the balance of power in the Far East and thereby endangered the interests of the Russian state:

> By the end of 1939, they (i.e. the Russians) supported the Kuomintang government against the Japanese and therefore against the Communists, for the arms Russia sent to Chiang would also be used against Mao's forces. As the rest of the world hesitated for fear of alienating Japan, Russia sent Chiang weapons. In the last two months of 1939 almost two-thirds of the arms shipped to Chiang through Rangoon were of Russian origin... Russia gave Chiang's governments vast credits, amounting to well over 50 million dollars by mid-1940...[3]

Subsequently, Stalin was equally accommodating with the Americans. He assured them that he wished to see a strong China united under Chiang's leadership. He ridiculed Mao and his followers, explaining to an American diplomat, "The Chinese communists are not real communists – they are 'margarine' communists".[4] At the same time, Stalin wrote to Mao, urging them to "unite with, be included in and under the National Government in China".[5] Mao at-

1. G. Kolko, op. cit., pp. 209-213.

2. *Ibid.*

3. G. Kolko, op. cit., p. 32.

4. Herbert Feis, *China Tangle*, p. 140. Presumably Stalin was one of these discerning politicians who could tell the difference between butter and margarine.

5. Herbert Feis, op. cit., pp. 271-3.

tempted to comply with Stalin's policy and opened unity negotiations with Chiang Kai-Shek. But such a course of action proved to be impossible: Chiang did not want cooperation but capitulation. Thus Mao and his followers were perforce compelled to fight – compelled to fight a regime which was so riddled with corruption it was unable to control. Nemesis for Chiang – the complete downfall of the Kuomintang on the Chinese mainland – came by 1949.

In all three types of situation instanced above – in Yugoslavia, Greece and China – the internal dynamics, the push of forces beyond Stalin's control, resulted in developments that the Kremlin bureaucracy did not want or encourage. It was only with the outbreak of the Cold War, when the Russian leaders wished to cause inconvenience to Western capitalism, that a switch of policy occurred. Only then did Stalin offer verbal (although not armed) support for the resistance in Greece and for Mao's campaign in China, or show some gratitude to Tito. These changes in policy were an effect of the Cold War rather than one of its causes.

Myth And Reality

The view that Russia in 1945 was hell-bent on world domination, and used the various Communist Parties as tools towards this end, is a myth that has been peddled in Western countries to justify rearmament. The truth is that Russia emerged from the Second World War in an extremely battered state, quite incapable of fighting a further global conflict. She had borne the brunt of struggle: for most of the war Russia was fighting 70-75% of the German army – Britain, America and the other allies fought the rest.[1] Consequently, Russian casualties were colossal, as Isaac Deutscher relates:

> *When, after the war, the first population census was carried out in the Soviet Union, it turned out that in the age groups that were older than 18 years at the end of the war, that is, in the whole adult population of the Soviet Union, there were only* 31 million men compared with 53 million women. *For many, many years only old men, cripples, children and women tilled the fields in the Russian countryside. Old women had to clear, with bare hands, the immense masses of rubble from their destroyed cities and towns. And this nation which had lost 20 million men in dead alone – and only think how many of the 31 million men that were left alive were the cripples and invalids and the wounded of the world war and how many were the old-aged – this nation with so tremendous, so huge a loss, this nation was supposed to threaten Europe with invasion!*[2]

However much they might whip up hysteria to deceive the masses, the overwhelming majority of Western politicians knew there was never the remotest

---

1. G. Kolko, op. cit., p. 19.
2. I. Deutscher's essay, 'Myths of the Cold War,' published in David Horowitz's book, *Containment or Revolution*, Blond, 1967. Emphasis in original.

chance of a Russian attack. Even the notorious John Foster Dulles admitted in one of his franker moments:

> *So far as it is humanly possible to judge, the Soviet Government, under condi-*
> *tions now prevailing, does not contemplate the use of war as an instrument of*
> *its national policy.* I do not know any responsible official, military or
> civilian, in this Government or any Government who believes that the
> Soviet Government now plans open military aggression.[1]

As one has to dismiss the charge against Russia, it is tempting to see the United States as entirely responsible for the Cold War. This explanation, which is frequently advanced by Communist Party supporters and fellow-travellers, has the virtue of simplicity. But such a uni-causal explanation, while containing an important element of truth, in my opinion does not lead to a full understanding of the highly complex international relationships that created the Cold War. There was a basic and fundamental incompatibility of America's and Russia's views of how the post-war world should develop.

The United States envisaged an international liberalisation. It wanted free trade and the right of business to invest anywhere in the world without let or hindrance. As the US State Department explained in 1944, 'This doctrine in its pure form would provide that the capital and enterprise of all countries should have equal opportunity (even with the capital and enterprise of the country in whose territories the resources existed) to participate in the ownership and development of natural resources'.[2] When the State Department talked of 'equal opportunity', it failed to add that some would be more equal than others. America, her economy expanded and strengthened by the war, would be very favourably placed compared to any other country.

Obviously, such a policy would give US capitalism hegemony over the world economy. A leading American statesman, Cordell Hull, openly recognised this fact when he said, "Leadership towards a new system of international relationships in trade and other economic affairs will devolve very largely upon the United States because of our great economic strength. We should assume this leadership, and the responsibility that goes with it, primarily for reasons of pure national self-interest".[3] It was a responsibility that Henry Wallace, the US vice-president, gleefully accepted. "The American business man of tomorrow," he said, would understand that "the new frontier extends from Minneapolis... all the way to Central Asia."[4]

But America's grandiose plans for post-war expansion conflicted with Russia's interests at three sensitive points. First, there was the question of defeated Germany. The Stalinist bureaucracy wanting to re-build Russia's ruined economy, favoured wholesale looting and plundering. The American politicians, on the other hand, recalled what happened to Germany after the First World

---

1. Cited David Horowitz, *From Yalta to Vietnam*. Emphasis added.
2. G. Kolko, op. cit., p. 254.
3. *Ibid*, p. 253.
4. *Ibid*.

War: stripping her of productive potential made it impossible for her to fulfil the reparation requirements of the Versailles Treaty Indeed, the United States, with its Dawes and Young Plans, had to pump more money into Germany than it obtained from Germany. Obviously, the US government did not want to see history repeat itself. It also had another reason for objecting to the Russian policy the growth and stability of European capitalism would be impossible without an economically viable Germany. All this meant that America's plans for long-term exploitation were not reconcilable with Russia's for short-term exploitation.

But the Stalinist bureaucracy's thirst for capital, the urgency of its need to accumulate, threw it into conflict with the United States in a second way. It proceeded to rifle Eastern Europe in a fashion that was reminiscent of the worst excesses of British imperialism in India and, in the course of its plundering, showed little concern for who happened to be the legal owner of the property they seized. Let me exemplify this point by taking the typical case of Rumania. In his book, *Stalin's Satellites in Europe*, Ygael Gluckstein wrote:

> *The most important machinery of the Ploesti Oil Refineries was dismantled by the Russian military authorities, and the Rumanians also had to hand over a fifth of the machinery of the textile and metallurgical industries... It has been estimated that in fact Rumania, from the armistice to June 1, 1948, paid the USSR $1,785 million in goods, etc.–a figure which would represent 84% of Rumania's national income for that period.[1]*

As this vicious and inhuman policy of the Stalinist bureaucracy stripped Rumania of anything of value, the plight of the Rumanian people became appalling, as the *Manchester Guardian* described:

> *the peasants are moving away in gangs in search of food, meanwhile eating grass and acorns and even chewing clay-bearing soil to assuage their hunger. They have slaughtered their cattle or bartered it for grain and have even, it is said, consumed seed corn although the authorities soaked it in oil before distributing it.[2]*

The American and British governments were not worried about the tremendous sufferings of the Rumanian people–their concern was simply limited to the fate of their investments. For only 15 to 20% of the capital of Rumanian industry was owned by Rumanians; the rest belonged to foreigners, mainly British, French and American capitalists.[3] So the Russian attack on Rumanian property was, by proxy, an attack on Anglo-American interests. This was resented by Western capitalists not only when it occurred in Rumania but also as it happened elsewhere in Eastern Europe.

---

1. Ygael Gluckstein (Tony Cliff), op. cit., p. 59.
2. *Manchester Guardian*, March 5th, 1947.
3. Royal Institute of International Affairs, *South-Eastern Europe: A Political and Economic Survey*, p. 173.

It was not merely that they lost large investments in the Balkans, but also that Americans were made to understand, by Russian conduct there, that the Stalinists' method of exploitation was diametrically opposed to their own. Their *modus operandi* – relying upon the state to extract the maximum surplus value – was incompatible with the American method of relying upon giant corporations to extend US influence. Indeed, Russian state regulation, extending into and dominating Eastern Europe, effectively roped this entire area off from the liberalisation of trade and investment which were an essential part of American post-war plans. Thus, a third source of conflict arose.

The Cold War should not be seen as a gigantic misunderstanding. Nor was it caused by the evil designs of any particular country or politician. But it developed because the imperialist interests of America and Russia did not coincide. Professor Kolko's book, in a magnificent fashion, gives a wealth of factual detail on the origins of the Cold War. Unfortunately, he does not possess the theoretical knowledge to underpin his argument to prove his point.

'... and so we call upon the occupied countries to rise against their oppressors – with the exception of India, of course!!'

Index

Lightning Source UK Ltd.
Milton Keynes UK
UKOW02f2323071216
289467UK00001B/13/P